DATE DUE

	JAN 1 1 1993	DEC 1 ⁷ 1992	

IMMIGRANTS ON THE THRESHOLD

IMMIGRANTS

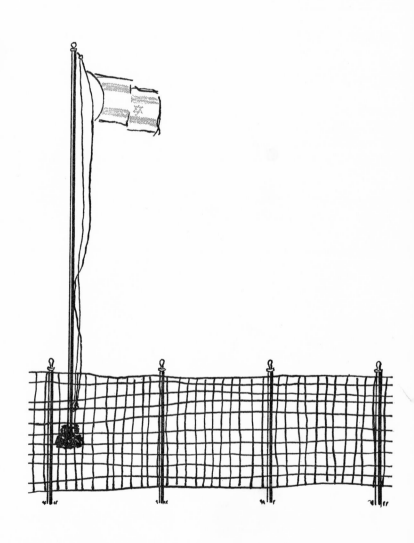

ON THE THRESHOLD
By Judith T. Shuval
Introduction by Louis Guttman

ATHERTON PRESS
A Division of Prentice-Hall, Inc.
70 Fifth Avenue
New York 11, New York

Published simultaneously
in Great Britain
by Prentice-Hall International
London

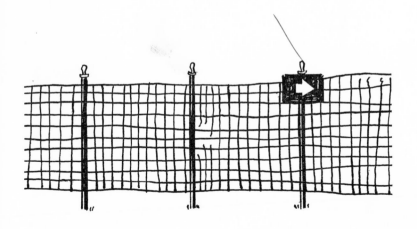

IMMIGRANTS ON THE THRESHOLD
Judith T. Shuval

Copyright © 1963 by Prentice-Hall, Inc.
Atherton Press, New York, New York

Published simultaneously in Great Britain by
Prentice-Hall International, Inc.
28 Welbeck Street, London W.1, England

Atherton Press, A Division of Prentice-Hall, Inc.
70 Fifth Avenue, New York 11, New York

Library of Congress Catalog Card Number 63-17467
Printed in the United States of America 45123

THE ATHERTON PRESS
BEHAVIORAL SCIENCE SERIES

General Editor
WILLIAM E. HENRY
The University of Chicago

Introduction

It may be trite to remark that the present is a transition point between the past and the future. Certain situations in the course of events, however, are sometimes singled out as indicating an interval of special significance between what came before and what will come after. Sometimes these situations are formally definable, such as the birth of a child or the day of a wedding ceremony; graduation from a high school or university in the United States is termed "commencement." The *bar mizvah* in the Jewish religion and similar rites in other cultures are taken to indicate that childhood is formally terminated and that from now on the boy is to be a responsible person in his own right. Less institutionalized interstitial periods occur idiosyncratically in the lives of individual persons and may often be judged turning points in their careers—the death of a loved one, promotion on the job, an inspiring lecture.

Introduction

Despite the ubiquity of social transitions in personal and group life, theory and research on the attending problems are scarce. Perhaps the most studied of such processes is adolescence. Although many of the problems encountered there may parallel those of adult life, there seems to be need for development of basic formulations directed immediately to adult problems.

Immigrants constitute a class of people for whom a relatively sharp division between past and future can be made. There is a fairly clearly demarcated point at which they physically enter their country of destination. Given such a physically clear transition point, one can begin to inquire about what it is in the past that helps them adjust to facing an unknown future. A more complete inquiry would be to follow them through the future— which would then turn into the past.

The extraordinary phenomenon of the recent immigration to Israel has made possible a deeply searching study of people in transit in this sense. In the following pages, Dr. Shuval reports on a study of almost two thousand immigrants from some twenty countries of origin during their first year in the new state of Israel. Through fortunate circumstances—from the research point of view—it was possible to make a cross-sectional study of a population during the vital transitional period. Presented here are the only data available, to the time of this writing, to give a representative picture of any sociopsychological problem of the immigrants to Israel as a whole. These data, in turn, are but a portion of a much larger collection which includes a cross-section of the entire population of Israel in 1949–1950. Again, these latter data are the only available on such a representative basis.

The data on which the present study is based were gathered in early months of the new state. The Israeli population as a whole—and apparently the Knesset (the Israeli parliament) in particular—was not too aware of the problems of absorbing the influx of thousands of immigrants in the short time following the War of Liberation. An enterprising young journalist for one of the leading daily Hebrew papers published a series of articles under the title "I Was an Immigrant for Thirty Days."

In Lincoln Steffens' fashion, he described conditions in the transit camps which had been hastily put up in various parts of the country as a temporary measure for handling the stream of immigrants. In the wake of the stir those articles caused, the government asked the Israel Institute of Applied Social Research to conduct an independent study, with no strings attached, of the adjustment of new immigrants to Israel. We designed the study completely at our own discretion, did the pretesting, and started the final field work. The government paid the monthly bills as they came in.

The field work was completed at a most unfortunate period in the government's history. The War of Liberation was finally over. Budgets that had been completely unbalanced had to become more realistic. The government was in a desperate financial state and overnight canceled hundreds of activities, including this research project. The data lay untouched until some sources of funds could be found. Despite the unusually rich data and the general importance of the problem, major support was not forthcoming from scientific foundations. The Marshall Field Foundation and the Lucius N. Littauer Foundation contributed toward the beginning of the tabulations, and they were finally completed with the aid of a subvention from UNESCO some ten years after the original field work.

The fact that in 1957 Judith T. Shuval was awarded the annual prize of the American Society for the Study of Social Problems for one of the chapters of the manuscript attests to the enduring importance of this work. The theoretical approach of the volume, the sociopsychological hypotheses formulated, and the conclusions reached are all substantial contributions to the general field of social psychology.

Much of the original data are not treated in the present work, and we hope that further publications will be possible. For example, an interesting and fundamental type of variable on which the data were gathered was personal adjustment. There is a great deal of discussion in the literature of immigration as to whether immigrants are less well adjusted or better adjusted than those who are not migrant. The interviews in the present study asked questions in this area, borrowed from work done on the adjustment of American soldiers during World War II.

At the suggestion of the present writer, the questions for the Army were developed by Prof. Leonard S. Cottrell in order to help the Research Branch of the Information and Education Division of the Army, with which we were then associated, distinguish between adjustment problems the enlistees had before entering the Army and adjustment problems arising from Army life.[1]

In the American Army studies it was not possible to take advantage of the notion of a zero point, since this was developed at the end of World War II. We cannot say what proportion of the American soldiers had positive personal adjustment and what proportion had negative personal adjustment. However, with the immigrants to Israel in the present study, the intensity-function technique for ascertaining a zero point enables us to say that approximately 80 per cent of the immigrants in the transit camps had positive personal adjustment and 20 per cent negative. Despite the sometimes indescribable conditions under which some of these people lived, on the whole they believed that they would get along well in the future.

An important part of the research design was the comparison of the immigrants with the old-time Jewish population of Palestine. Too few studies in social science make use of such a control-group technique. The immigrant interviews were run parallel with interviews among a cross section of the entire Jewish population in all parts of the country. Interestingly enough, again about 80 per cent was found to have positive personal adjustment. In this respect the immigrants in transit did not basically differ from the settled population. In a more specialized study made in 1954 among the *kibbutzim* of Israel (to our knowledge, the only cross-sectional study ever made of the *kibbutzim*), the questions on adjustment were asked again,

---

[1] Samuel A. Stouffer *et al., The American Soldier: Adjustment During Army Life* (Princeton: Princeton University Press, 1949), and *idem, Measurement and Prediction* (Princeton: Princeton University Press, 1950).

and again approximately 80 per cent had positive adjustment. The immigrants in transit differ from the settled population and *kibbutz* members quite markedly on certain areas of adjustment, but not on the basic sociopsychological one of personal adjustment.

Dr. Shuval has taken a different point of departure for her analysis. She has gone more deeply into certain aspects of the data and has come up with some remarkable findings of potential generalized importance. Her basic emphasis has been to distinguish *within* the immigrants in transit the variables which lead to quicker or slower acculturation.

Dr. Shuval's methodology has basically been that of studying the simultaneous relationships among certain triplets of variables. Specifically, her procedure is to hypothesize that, if a particular variable of the triplet is held constant, the relationships between the other two variables will possibly be explicated. Thus, her study is of the conditional correlations between two variables when a third is held constant.

Apart from the sociopsychological importance of the empirical findings, several of the statistical tables that Dr. Shuval presents may well serve as important examples to be studied by students of social research and statistics. Too often students are left with the impression that the study of partial correlation invariably leads to a single coefficient which is *the* coefficient of partial correlation. We are not always made aware of the assumptions of homogeneity under which only a single coefficient obtains. Sociopsychological phenomena are often far too complex to fulfill the simple conditions taught in the usual course on statistics. This was pointed out many years ago in my "Outline of the Statistical Theory of Prediction." [2] Paul Lazarsfeld, too, has long emphasized this in advocating the term "conditional correlation" instead of the term "partial correlation." For each category of the variable held constant, a different kind of relationship between the remaining two variables may hold.

In the chapter "Ideology and Decision-Making," Dr. Shuval

[2] In Paul Horst *et al., The Prediction of Personal Adjustment* (New York: Social Science Research Council, 1941).

holds the variable "Zionism" constant. The two variables whose relations are then studied are "information about Israel" and "plans for settlement." The findings are that among Zionists there is a positive relation between the two variables, whereas among non-Zionists the correlation is negative. Here we have a striking example of two conditional correlations being opposite for the same triplet of variables. One cannot speak of *the* partial correlation here.

Another important example of conditional correlations relates to the "hardening" hypothesis of Chapter 6. The constant is experience in a Nazi concentration camp. This time, it is the magnitude, not the direction, of the correlation which changes with the condition. Among those who had not been in concentration camps, there is a substantial correlation between difficulties in Israel and pessimism about the future in Israel. Among those who did have experience in concentration camps, the correlation is generally relatively small.

The conditional-correlation methodology has the profound property of affording a point of departure for arriving at generalizations concerning similar social processes in other contexts. In the first of the above examples, replace "Zionism" by the general concept "desire to adapt." A paradigm might be suggested to express the hypothesized conditional correlations: in a new situation requiring adaptation, those who already have a desire to adapt will find it easier to decide what to do the more information they have; for those who do not desire to adapt, the difficulty in deciding what to do will increase with the amount of information they have. Stated this way, the paradigm depicts the problem of immigrants as one special case of the transition problem. It may be valuable to see whether the paradigm holds for other transitional periods. The paradigm for hardening can be similarly restated in general terms, as can most of the other findings on the acculturation of the immigrants to Israel.

In the early days of our Institute, which is now in its fifteenth year, we liked to point out that Israel was an ideal laboratory for social research. And, indeed, many others have enthusiastically made the same observation. But, as the years go by, we have come to realize that a laboratory does not arise full-grown in response to natural research opportunities. A laboratory requires scientists, facilities, and support. Unfortunately, in neither the Institute nor elsewhere in the country do we have enough of these to consolidate and integrate the advances we have made. In particular, the time has come to reanalyze the data from some two hundred studies to see what systematic picture can be thereby obtained. Such secondary analyses are important and relatively inexpensive functions of a research establishment and have resulted elsewhere in major scientific publications.

All the more welcome, therefore, is the present work of Judith T. Shuval. It provides a sound empirical baseline for the period shortly after the founding of the state. Studies of later periods can use this volume as a basis for comparison, so that social change can be charted through time. New and more systematic field work needs to be done in the near future, so that this opportunity to contribute to the knowledge of social change is not wasted. Let us hope that the present volume is only the first of a series of equally well-integrated works of theory, hypothesis-testing, and large-scale field work.

Louis Guttman
Scientific Director
The Israel Institute of Applied Social Research

Preface

I am indebted to several people and institutions in the preparation of this volume. My deepest obligation is to Louis Guttman, scientific director of the Israel Institute of Applied Social Research, who played a crucial role in helping to sharpen my sense of scientific rigor through many hours of discussion and analysis of the problems raised by the data. More than any other person, he is probably responsible for whatever merit this book may possess, although it goes without saying that he is in no way responsible for its shortcomings. His generosity in placing the scientific, technical, and administrative facilities of the Institute at my disposal for long periods of time is hereby most gratefully acknowledged.

Many people on the staff of the Israel Institute of Applied Social Research had a part in the preparation of this book. My earliest debt is to the field workers, almost all of whom were recent immigrants, who carried out the interviews on which the analysis is primarily based. Knowing that they worked in the transit camps when transportation was difficult and living conditions were trying, I am more than aware of their devotion and loyalty. During the period between the actual data collection and the final revisions of the manuscript, the scientific and technical staff of the Institute constantly assisted and encouraged me. In particular, Uzi Haim, chief of the Data Processing Section, was indefatigable in supplying me with what might have appeared to be endless requests for tabulations and statistical analyses. Rachel Hendly, administrative officer of the Institute, was always more than helpful in easing the many administrative problems of carrying out the study.

I am indebted to the Marshall Field Foundation and to the Lucius N. Littauer Foundation for financial support during the early stages of the study. Financial support for the final preparation of the manuscript for publication was given by UNESCO as part of its program of aid to member states. Under its auspices, I held the post of adviser in social research at the Institute during 1956–1957. I was thus able to devote myself fully to writing the results of the study.

Several social scientists read all or part of the manuscript at various stages of its development. I am indebted to all of them for their fruitful and insightful comments, and it goes without saying that they are in no way responsible for any of its weaknesses. Elihu Katz was most generous in spending many hours in stimulating discussions of the problems raised by the study. I am especially grateful to him for the time and insight he gave to the analysis. S.N. Eisenstadt and Yonina Garber-Talmon also contributed several useful comments and suggestions.

Portions of this study have appeared in the journals in somewhat different versions. A paper entitled "Some Persistent Effects of Trauma: Five Years After the Nazi Concentration Camps" received the Helen L. DeRoy Award for 1957, which is given by the Society for the Study of Social Problems. This paper was published in *Social Problems*, V, No. 3 (1957–1958). The material on which it was based here appears in Chapter 6. Some of the material in Chapter 4 appeared in a paper entitled "The Role of Ideology as a Predisposing Frame of Reference for Immigrants" in *Human Relations,* XII, No. 1 (1959). Portions of Chapters 7 and 10 appeared in *The American Sociological Review* and *Sociometry* in 1963.

Most important is my debt to Hillel without whose encouragement and support this volume would not have been written. Rama and Tami also contributed to the study, each in her own way.

Judith T. Shuval

Jerusalem
1963

Contents

Introduction vii

Preface xv

List of Tables xxi

One · Opening 1
1. *The Setting* 3
2. *The Framework* 22
3. *History and Methods* 33

Two · Response to Strain 43
4. *Ideology and Decision-Making* 45
5. *Ideology and Frustration* 64
6. *The Nazi Concentration Camp* 79
7. *Unemployment and Morale* 104

Contents

Three · First Gropings at Acculturation 115
       8. *Early Patterns of Acculturation* 117

Four · Orientation to the Future 139
       9. *Occupational Aspirations* 141
     10. *Aspirations for Mobility* 155

Five · Closing 175
    11. *Conclusions* 177

Appendix A · The Questionnaire 195
Appendix B · Sampling Procedure 210
Index 213

List of Tables

No.	Title	Page
1	Number of Jewish Immigrants to Israel by Year of Immigration and Continent of Birth	14
2	Ethnic Groups in the Population Sample	31
3	Percentage of "Better Informed" among Immigrants of Differing Zionist Backgrounds and Lengths of Time in Israel	53
4	Percentage of "Better Informed" Related to Zionist Background, Length of Time in Israel, and Education	55
5	Plans for Settlement, Related to Zionist Background and Level of Information	56
6	Plans for Settlement, Related to Zionist Background, Level of Information, and Educational Background	58

7   Disappointment with Israel as a Function of Zionist
       Background and Ethnic Origin   67
8   Accuracy of Information   69
9   Disappointment with Israel as a Function of In-
       formation, Zionist Background, and Ethnic
       Origin   71
10   Psychosomatic Complaints as a Function of Disap-
       pointment with Israel and Zionist Background   73
11   Feelings of Exploitation, Related to Disappoint-
       ment with Israel and Zionist Background   75
12   Comparison of Concentration Camp Survivors and
       Control Population   86
13   Effect of Strain on Immigrants' Level of Optimism   91
14   Orientation toward Future of Concentration Camp
       Survivors and Control Population in Situations
       Not Conducive to Strain   93
15   Orientation toward Future in Response to Failure
       to Receive Assistance in Settlement among
       Concentration Camp Survivors and Control
       Population   94
16   Orientation toward Future in Response to Disap-
       pointment with Israel among Concentration
       Camp Survivors and Control Population   95
17   Orientation toward Future in Relation to Length
       of Time in the Immigrant Camp among Con-
       centration Camp Survivors and Control Popu-
       lation   96
18   Orientation toward Future in Relation to Family
       Tension among Concentration Camp Survivors
       and Control Population   98
19   Psychosomatic Complaints of Concentration Camp
       Survivors and Control Population   101
20   Perception of Hostility in the Outside World and
       Feeling of Exploitation among Concentration
       Camp Survivors and Control Population   102
21   Morale as a Function of Unemployment among
       Groups Differing in Ethnic Background, Age,

	Length of Time in Israel, and Education	106
22	Morale as a Function of Unemployment among Groups Differing in Ethnic Background and Length of Time in Israel	107
23	Morale, Employment, and the Transit Camp as a Comparative Reference Group	111
24	Length of Time in Israel	123
25	Acceptance of Ideal Norms Related to Time and Ethnicity	124
26	Sources of Advice and Information Related to Time and Ethnic Background	125
27	Attitude toward Host Society	126
28	Morale Variables	130
29	Orientation toward Future, Disappointment with Israel, and Personal Adjustment, as Related to Time and Ethnic Background	131
30	Desire to Emigrate, Feeling of Exploitation, and Psychosomatic Disturbances, as Related to Time and Ethnic Background	132
31	Effects over Time of Orientation toward Future on Acculturation Variables	134
32	Summary of Effects over Time of Six Morale Variables on Acculturation Variables	135
33	Immigrants' Choices of Occupations for Their Eldest Sons	144
34	Rank of Occupations Chosen for Sons	145
35	Occupations Chosen by Men and Women Immigrants	146
36	Choice of Crafts and Trades by Sex, Age, and Education	147
37	Choice of White-Collar and Army Jobs by Sex, Ethnic Background, and Education	148
38	Choice of the Professions by Sex, Ethnic Background, Education, and Age	149
39	Effect of Zionism on Occupational Aspirations by Ethnic Background and Sex	150
40	Effect of Immigrants' Orientation toward the Future	

	on Occupational Aspirations by Ethnic Background and Sex	151
41	Effect of Zionism and Orientation toward Future on Choice of Agriculture and *Kibbutz*	153
42	Fathers' Occupations Before Immigrating to Israel	159
43	Choices of Occupations by Immigrant Fathers for Their Eldest Sons	160
44	Direction of Mobility of Fathers' Occupational Aspirations for Their Sons	162
45	Effects of Ethnic Origin, Age, Education, and Length of Time in Israel on Occupational Aspirations	163
46	Effect of Employment Status on Occupational Mobility	165
47	Effect of Activity-Passivity on Occupational Aspirations	166
48	Effect of Activity-Passivity on Occupational Aspirations among Class and Ethnic Groups	167
49	Activity as Related to Ethnic Background, Education, and Length of Time in Israel	169

One · Opening

1 · The Setting

The immigrants with which this study deals arrived in Israel during the height of immigration to the newly established state, the first two years of its existence. Immediately upon its establishment in May, 1948, Israel proclaimed an open-door–immigration policy as one of its cardinal tenets. The lifting of the severe restrictions on immigration imposed by the British Mandatory authorities resulted in an immediate influx of Jews from many parts of the world. This book concerns these immigrants between 1949 and 1950, their first year in Israel.

IMMIGRATION

In order to gain perspective on the group of immigrants with whom we shall deal, it is useful to consider certain aspects of the problem of immigration to Palestine in historical terms.[1]

[1] For a fuller discussion of the history of Jewish immigration to Palestine, see Joseph Dunner, *The Republic of Israel* (New York and London: McGraw-

Two dominant elements of pre-state immigration are of particular relevance to an understanding of the mass immigration to Israel. The first of these concerns the central place of immigration in the ideological value system of the Yishuv, the pre-state Jewish population of Palestine. The second concerns the restrictive immigration policy of the Palestine government, in particular the British Mandatory authorities. The interplay of these two elements goes far in explaining the phenomenon of mass immigration after the establishment of Israel.

The establishment of the state of Israel represented the culmination of fifty years of political and ideological striving, but a much longer history of hope and yearning of the Jewish people for the re-establishment of their ancient homeland. This yearning had been expressed in the prayers and traditional literature for hundreds of years; orthodox Jews never gave up hope of returning to Jerusalem and of restoring the ancient religious institutions there. The new state was thus viewed by practically all Jews, religious and secular, as a historical achievement of the highest order. It was greeted with emotion and enthusiasm as the historic fulfillment of generations of hope and fifty years of active political effort.[2]

Zionist ideology during the post-Herzl period has tradi-

Hill Book Company, Inc., 1950); S. N. Eisenstadt, *The Absorption of Immigrants* (London: Routledge & Kegan Paul, Ltd., 1954), chaps. 2, 3, 4; ESCO Foundation for Palestine, *Palestine: A Study of Jewish, Arab, and British Policies* (New Haven: ESCO, 1947); Oscar I. Janowsky, *Foundations of Israel* (Princeton, N.J.: D. Van Nostrand Company, Inc., 1959); Hal Lehrman, *Israel: The Beginning and Tomorrow* (New York: William Sloane Associates, 1948); Harry Sacher, *Israel: The Establishment of a State* (London: George Weidenfeld and Nicholson, 1952); Moshe Sicron, *Immigration to Israel 1948–1953* (Jerusalem: Falk Project for Economic Research in Israel and the Central Bureau of Statistics, 1957), chap. II; Judith T. Shuval, "Patterns of Inter-Group Tension and Affinity," *International Social Science Bulletin*, VIII, No. 1 (1956), 75–123.

[2] For a discussion of Zionist ideology and the central place of immigration in its system of values see Martin Buber, *Israel and Palestine: The History of an Idea* (New York: Farrar, Strauss and Young, Inc., 1952); Israel Cohen, *The Zionist Movement* (London: Frederick Muller, Ltd., 1945); Isaac Gruenbaum, *The History of Zionism* (Tel Aviv: The Zionist Library, Zionist Organization Youth Department, 1946); Ben Halpern, *The Idea of a Jewish State* (Cambridge, Mass.: Harvard University Press, 1961).

tionally emphasized physical settlement in Palestine as the major solution to the Jewish problem. Despite the fact that the actual number of settlers was not always large, immigration has been a dominant end of the ideology from the earliest period of the political movement. In the face of the many political obstacles that confronted the Zionist movement, physical settlement through immigration became the central goal toward which energies were directed.

Immigration assumed an even more crucial place in the ideology during the 1930's, when the Nazi persecution of the Jews began. From this period on the importance of immigration for the Zionist movement expanded from an ideological value to an affectively toned end which was viewed as crucial in saving thousands of lives. The latter emphasis, which reached its climax during the period immediately preceding the establishment of the state, transformed free immigration into a dominant theme in the life of the entire Yishuv. It was perhaps the most widely spread and emotionally colored value of the pre-state Jewish population, many of whom had families in Nazi-dominated Europe.

The policy of restricted immigration imposed by the British Mandatory authorities served to further reinforce the dominant theme of free immigration. The White Paper of 1939 authorized the entry of only 75,000 immigrants over a five-year period; however, conditions in Europe and Palestine being what they were, only 54,000 immigrants, legal and illegal, entered Palestine between 1939 and 1943.[3] The severe official restrictions during the period of the Nazi holocaust raised the value of free immigration to an almost frenzied height, resulting in mass participation of the Yishuv in widespread efforts at illegal immigration.

At the time Israel was established in 1948, the themes of free immigration in the value system of the Yishuv and restrictive-immigration policy of the British authorities had combined to raise free immigration to the apex of the hierarchy of values of

[3] Sicron, *op. cit.*, p. 23; ESCO Foundation for Palestine, *op. cit.*; *The Political History of Palestine under British Administration, Memorandum by His Britannic Majesty's Government*, presented in July, 1947, to the United Nations Special Committee on Palestine (Jerusalem: 1947).

the Jewish population of Palestine. It is, therefore, not surprising that one of the first official acts of the newly established provisional government was to institute a policy of completely free immigration for as many Jews as chose to immigrate to the new state. This policy was an unrestricted one, permitting almost all types of people, even those requiring public support of one sort or another, to enter. *Kibbutz Galuyot,* the "in-gathering of the exiles" became a cardinal tenet of the new state.

The first burst of enthusiastic free immigration resulted in a great strain to the social system because of the admission of large numbers of aged, chronically ill, and other people who became public burdens in the welfare institutions. It is of some interest to note that within a few years this policy was, of necessity, modified to one of selective immigration, so that the physical fitness and potential economic independence of possible immigrants were evaluated before immigration. At the same time, the principle of free immigration has remained one of the central values of the social system and is re-invoked whenever Jews in any part of the world are in physical peril. It goes almost without saying, for example, that, were the Soviet Union to allow Jews to emigrate, a policy of completely unrestricted immigration would be put into effect no matter what the economic or social hardships to Israel. The period with which we deal in this study represents the height of the unrestricted-immigration policy immediately after the establishment of the state, when the ideological pressures, as well as the population pressures from the D.P. (displaced persons) camps and the Arab countries, were at their maximum.

The result of the early open-door policy was a mass immigration from Europe, the D.P. camps, and the Arab countries such as few countries have experienced. From May 15, 1948, to December 31, 1948, 101,828 immigrants arrived in Israel; in 1949, 239,567; in 1950, 170,249; and in 1951, 175,095.[4]

In 1952 immigration began to fall off and rose again only in 1956, when large numbers of immigrants began coming from Poland, Hungary, and North Africa.[5] The overwhelming size of

[4] Sicron, *op. cit.,* Table 2, p. 45.

[5] The number of immigrants during the years following the mass immigra-

the immigration during the early years of the state's existence is made graphic if one considers that the Jewish population of Palestine at the time of the establishment of Israel was only 649,633; after approximately three and one-half years, the population had doubled.

The economic and social problems involved in the absorption of such a large population were enormous, especially for a new state which had just come through a war and had not yet had time to establish appropriate institutions to undertake such an overwhelming task. The most immediate problems were employment and housing; the questions of full social and cultural absorption remained more in the realm of long-term problems. The shortage of investment capital during the first years of the state's existence made the provision of employment opportunities for immigrants extremely difficult, and the result was widespread unemployment. The housing shortage, which had persisted since World War II, was partially alleviated during 1948, when 117,000 immigrants found shelter in abandoned Arab dwellings. However, at the beginning of 1949, it became necessary to establish transit camps on a wide scale. By the end of April, 1949, there were twenty-four such camps housing close to 60,000 immigrants; by the end of April, 1950, there were 95,000 immigrants living in thirty-five transit camps in various parts of the country. During the summer of 1950, the Jewish Agency instituted a new policy of temporary immigrant settlement, the *ma'abara,* in which an attempt was made to encourage residents to obtain employment, even if on a limited scale, in order to become self-supporting.[6]

tion were 1952, 24,369; 1953, 11,326; 1954, 18,500; 1955, 37,500; 1956, over 50,000. The immigration restrictions were associated mainly with Israel's economic difficulties and with the restrictions placed on emigration from east European countries. At the end of 1951, the Jewish Agency introduced an immigration policy of medical and occupational selection. *Ibid.,* pp. 35, 45, 121.

[6] On certain organizational aspects of immigrant settlement during this period, see *Government of Israel Year Book, 1949–50* (Jerusalem: Government Printer, 1950) and *Government of Israel Year Book, 1950–51* (Jerusalem: Government Printer, 1951), articles on immigrant absorption. Sacher, *op. cit.;* and Janowsky, *op. cit.*

THE TRANSIT CAMP

The present study focuses on the interim period during which the immigrants who arrived in 1949 and 1950 were still living in the transit camps. Although only a transitional stage in the absorption process, this first picture of the immigrant and his initial reaction to the reality of his new country is aimed at gaining some insight into the earliest aspects of adjustment and acculturation. The policy of immigrant settlement has changed with experience and the improved economic stability of the country, the transit camp shortly giving way to the *ma'abara* and, when the housing shortage was less acute, the *ma'abara* giving way to the ship-to-settlement policy. Although the last mentioned policy has been in effect during recent years, the procedure of the period of heaviest immigration is of more than historic interest. Any society suddenly faced with the need to absorb a mass influx of immigrants would probably be forced to use some sort of a transit camp procedure during the first stages of settlement because no society has the means and facilities in its institutional structure to cope with the sort of emergency measures which mass immigration calls for. The transit camp acts as a temporary absorbing mechanism until other institutions can be adjusted. The pheonomenon of the transit camp is, therefore, of considerable general interest from the point of view of large-scale immigration problems. In effect, camps serve as the principal means of immediate absorption in Australia and other countries which have admitted large numbers of immigrants. Furthermore, it is possible that even Israel itself might again be faced with mass immigration should, for example, the Soviet Union suddenly allow Jewish emigration. Despite the improved methods of settlement which have been developed with experience in Israel, a really large-scale immigration might well impose such strain on the social system that something akin to the transit camps of 1949 and 1950 would be necessary.

Furthermore, I believe that many of the problems studied here are not necessarily a direct function of the type of organizational setting in which the immigrant is placed. The effect of

8

experience in a Nazi concentration camp, the role played by Zionist ideology, the reaction to unemployment in terms of relevant reference groups are all sociological processes which are of interest in themselves in terms of the broader aspects of immigrant adjustment. They can be studied in the transit camp, as well as in any other form of initial settlement, without obscuring much of the fundamental structure of the process. It is true, of course, that we must constantly bear in mind that we are dealing with the earliest impact of the new society on the immigrant in a temporary setting that is undoubtedly quite different from that of his ultimate setting. However, this should not make certain basic problems less amenable to study. Unfortunately, in the absence of a comparative immigrant population, we are unable to separate the effect of the transit camp from the possible effects of other modes of initial settlement.

Finally, this historic fact should not be forgotten: the immigrant transit camp served as the initial mode of reception for some 150,000 immigrants in 1949–1950, during the height of the mass immigration to Israel. This mode of temporary settlement was typical for a considerable proportion of the new arrivals and is, therefore, of intrinsic interest in itself. What is more, the *ma'abara* form of settlement, which was instituted in the middle of 1950, was not too different from the transit camp in many of its structural aspects. True, there were no public eating facilities, each family arranging for its own cooking; there was somewhat more privacy in the dwelling units; and families were generally more independent than they were in the camps. However, in their isolation from the mainstream of Israeli life, in the widespread unemployment which characterized most of them, in the bleak tent or tin hut accommodations, and in the minimal facilities for social life and recreation the *ma'abara* was not too different from the transit camp. This was particularly true during the early stages of *ma'abara* settlement. In some cases the change-over was more in name than in physical setting, for the authorities simply closed down the public kitchens and certain other services and proclaimed the transit camp a *ma'abara* as of a certain date. The principal object of the change in settlement policy

9

from transit camps to the *ma'abara* was to stop the immigrants' dependence on public agencies for support. Although this end was, to a large extent, attained, the physical and social setting of the *ma'abara* did not present too different a picture from the transit camp.

What was the immigrant transit camp like? [7] Most of the transit camps were established in former British army camps. At the time Israel was established, there were only seven transit camps housing some 7,000 immigrants. By the end of April, 1950, however, there were some 90,000 immigrants living in thirty-five camps in various parts of the country. Under the extreme pressure of a rapidly growing immigrant population, the initial function of the transit camp—to house the immigrant for a few days, give him a medical examination, classify him for employment and housing opportunities—was quickly changed to one of fairly long-term housing, often lasting six months to a year.

At first, housing was in army barracks with makeshift partitions between family units. However, when all the barracks were occupied, tents were put up for the excess population. By the middle of 1950, over half of the camp population was living in tents. Conditions were crowded, with large families occupying a single room. Sanitary facilities were located outside the living quarters. Families had no private cooking facilities; food was provided without cost at public dining halls. Many families, however, preferred to eat in privacy and used to line up at the kitchen to get their food, then eat it in their living quarters. Few of the transit camps had any landscaping to break the sordid monotony of row after row of barracks or tents.

The physical bleakness of the camps was increased by the widespread unemployment, which left hundreds of unoccupied people, time hanging heavily on their hands, lounging about the camp. The economy of the country had not yet been adjusted to provide employment for large numbers of immigrants, and the camps, often located in isolated parts of the country, were not

---

[7] On this subject see article on "Immigration and Absorption," *Government of Israel Year Book, 1950–51, op. cit.*

always accessible to the employment opportunities that existed. In addition, there was a certain reluctance on the part of many men to work at low-paying, status-losing jobs when they and their families were being supported at public expense in the transit camp. It was basically this problem that initiated the change in settlement policy. The women, having very limited household responsibilities and no cooking facilities, were also unemployed, and time hung heavily on their hands, too. Outside employment opportunities for women were equally, if not more, limited in a period of general unemployment. The general inactivity and stagnation were reinforced by the fact that the school and kindergarten facilities, although formally established in most camps, were so crowded and operated so irregularly that the camps were overrun with unoccupied children of all ages.

The Jewish Agency was officially responsible for running the immigrant transit camps.[8] Representatives of the Agency maintained office hours in each of the camps for consultation with immigrants who wanted or needed advice on settlement problems. Getting to see one of these officials was usually a tedious process for the immigrant and the harassed officials, involving hours of waiting and frequent battles over privileges which the immigrant felt were his due. The Jewish Agency, in cooperation with several of the women's social service organizations, maintained kindergartens and baby clinics in the camps; the Ministry of Health maintained public clinics and hospital facilities. In most of the camps there were also popularly elected immigrant committees, the function of which was to cooperate with the authorities in running the various services with a measure of democratic self-government. These committees did not always function as effectively as might have been desired because of inter-ethnic tensions and many immigrants' lack of experience with the procedures of self-government.

The over-all picture of the transit camp would not be complete without noting its extreme isolation from the mainstream

---

[8] For a general description of the Jewish Agency and its functions, see Janowsky, *op. cit.*, pp. 34–37, and Sacher, *op. cit.*, pp. 41–43.

of Israeli life. Not only were many of the camps located at some distance from the main population centers, but, even when they were not physically isolated, a certain social isolation of newly arrived immigrants from the old-timers in the community was very marked. It was during this period that the press coined the now widespread terms "first Israel" and "second Israel" to refer to the relatively privileged old-timers and the isolated, under-privileged immigrants. The use of these two names emphasized the separation of the two groups. Even for the minority of im-migrants who were fortunate enough to find jobs, the work situa-tion generally did not provide the sort of equalitarian relation-ship with old-timers which might foster meaningful social con-tact, for the latter usually occupied positions of authority, whereas the immigrants were, more often than not, unskilled laborers. Inadequate and crowded public transportation facilities further emphasized the isolation of the camps. Furthermore, during this period the public bodies and welfare organizations which might have concerned themselves with alleviating the isolation of im-migrants were so overburdened with the vast physical problems of a mass immigration that the social and psychological problems were considered far less urgent.

In addition to their isolation from the old-time Israeli com-munity, immigrants were, to a large extent, cut off from familiar social contacts and primary relationships which play such a cru-cial role in the individual's system of security and well-being. Of necessity, the mass immigration separated families and friends. Such separation was probably a particularly severe blow to the immigrants from traditional cultures, in which extended-family relationships are strongly maintained. There are no systematic data on this subject, but it is my impression that the extremely overcrowded public buses indicated that the immigrants were con-stantly on the move, seeking relatives and friends either among old-time settlers or in other immigrant camps. The crowded buses were only one external symptom of the extreme isolation the immigrants felt during their initial period in Israel.

Some empirical evidence is available concerning immigrants' lack of contact with the larger social system through the mass media. For example, only 19 per cent of the immigrants read a newspaper at least three or four times a week, whereas 81 per cent of the old-timers reported that they did. Only 18 per cent of the immigrants listened to the radio almost every day, whereas 74 per cent of the old-timers did. With respect to movies, lectures, and theater attendance, the differences between the two groups are equally striking: 21 per cent of the immigrants, compared to 60 per cent of the old-timers, attended the movies at least once or twice a month even though they were available in the transit camps; 19 per cent of the immigrants, compared to 31 per cent of the old-timers, reported that they attended public lectures once or twice a month; 6 per cent of the immigrants, compared to 79 per cent of the old-timers, had seen at least one Hebrew play. These differences indicate the extreme isolation of the immigrants during their first year in Israel.

The result of this twofold isolation, from the old-time community on the one hand and from familiar social contacts on the other, forced the residents of the transit camps very much into themselves; life focused essentially in the camp, rather than in the community outside it. This was not because life in the camp had much to recommend it, but simply because of the lack of any alternative.

THE IMMIGRANT POPULATION

Immigrants to Israel came from far and wide, from a large assortment of countries and cultures.[9] During the eight months of 1948 (the state was established in May), the majority of immigrants were from Poland, Rumania, and Bulgaria, but there was also a considerable number from North Africa (Algeria, Morocco, Tunisia, Libya) and Turkey.

The earliest arrivals of 1948 and some of those who came at the beginning of 1949 obtained housing in abandoned Arab property and did not live in the transit camps. We shall, therefore, be concerned only with the immigrants who arrived during parts of 1949 and 1950.[10] During 1949 and 1950, the proportion

[9] The data in this section are drawn from Sicron, *op. cit.*

[10] Sampling and interviewing did not cover all the immigrants who arrived

of European immigrants decreased considerably while the percentage from Asia and Africa increased markedly (see Table 1). In 1949, there were still groups arriving from Poland, Rumania, Bulgaria, Czechoslovakia, and Hungary; immigration from Yemen reached its peak during this year (35,138), as did the immigration from Turkey (26,295) and North Africa (39,135).[11] Thus it may be seen that the proportion from Asia increased from 5 per cent to almost 31 per cent between 1948 and 1949 while the proportion from Africa grew from 9 per cent to almost 17 per cent. During the same period the proportion from Europe decreased from 85 per cent to only about 50 per cent: the entire ethnic composition of the immigrant population had changed.

TABLE 1

NUMBER OF JEWISH IMMIGRANTS TO ISRAEL BY YEAR OF IMMIGRATION AND CONTINENT OF BIRTH *

	1948	1949	1950
Total number	101,828	239,576	170,249
Percentage			
Asia	5.3	30.6	34.4
Africa	9.1	16.7	15.2
Europe	85.1	52.1	49.8
America and Oceania	0.5	0.6	0.6

* Taken from Sicron, *op. cit.*, p. 45, Table 2.

1950 was the year of the mass immigration from Rumania (46,178), Iraq (32,453), and Iran (10,519). During this year, immigration from Poland (26,499) and North Africa (18,756) also

during 1949 and 1950, but began in the winter of 1949 and ended in the spring of 1950. Thus the data from Sicron are not entirely comparable to our sample population. See Chapter 3 and Appendix B for details of the sampling and interviewing procedures.

[11] The immigration from North Africa in 1949 was distributed as follows: 7,145 from Egypt, 17,924 from Algeria, Tunisia, and Morocco, and 14,066 from other North African countries, mainly Libya. See *Government of Israel Year Book, 1950–51, op. cit.*, Statistical Annual, Table 6.

continued, although on a somewhat diminished scale. However, the proportion of arrivals from Africa, Asia, and Europe remained approximately the same as in the previous year. In terms of the present study, it should be noted that most of the Iraqi and Iranian immigrants of 1950 arrived too late in the year to be included in our sample. Members of ethnic groups who arrived within a few months of one another were often housed together in camp facilities available at the time. This often resulted in ethnic concentrations of immigrants in certain camps. The Yemenites had to undergo certain medical check-ups and were, therefore, housed together in separate transit camps. Owing to circumstances beyond my control, they also are not included in the present study.

The immigrants who arrived in Israel after the establishment of the state differed in age from immigrants to other countries of the world and from the immigrants who had arrived in Palestine during the Mandate period. Compared to immigrants to other countries, immigrants to Israel were characterized by a higher proportion of children (fourteen and under) and a lower proportion of people in the early working ages (fifteen to thirty-nine). The proportion of aged people does not differ much from that of immigrants to other countries. The same general differences exist when we compare immigrants who arrived after the establishment of the state with those who arrived during the Mandate period: there were more young children and fewer people in the early working ages. In addition, the recent arrivals were characterized by a slightly higher proportion of aged people as compared to the pre-state immigrants. These changes are accounted for by the high percentage of children among Asian and African immigrants, compared to European immigrants, owing to the higher birth rate among the former and the absence of children and young people in Nazi Europe during the war. In the early working ages, the proportion of Europeans exceeds that of the Asian and African groups.

The sex ratio of the immigrants was approximately balanced. During the first year of the state, when many young pioneers arrived, males exceeded females, but in subsequent years the

15

ratio of the two sexes became more balanced. This over-all balance did not exist within all the ethnic and age subgroups of the population, but represents an average picture of the total population. The differences in sex ratio among the ethnic groups are associated with their different age structures, since all the groups show a preponderance of males in the younger age groups; among the North Africans, for example, with their preponderance of children, there is a sex ratio favoring males, whereas among the Europeans, where the proportion of elderly people is greater, the reverse is the case. In addition, Youth Aliyah brought more young boys than girls from Africa, since the latter were less easily separated from their families.[12]

Immigration during the early years of the state consisted, to a large extent, of a transfer of entire communities to Israel. This resulted in a fairly normal family structure corresponding to that of the Jewish communities in the various countries of origin. Compared to the veteran population of the country, the immigrants are characterized by a higher proportion of unmarried people, and a considerably higher percentage of widowed. Among the several ethnic groups, the proportion of married people at any age level is always greater among the Asians and Africans than it is among the Europeans. The only exception to this rule occurs among the Iraqi immigrants, among whom there are practically no differences from the Europeans. The average size of the immigrant family increased after the establishment of the state: this was because of the large number of Asian and African immigrant families, which are generally characterized by large numbers of children. The average family size among Asians and Africans was 4.0, whereas it was only 2.8 among the Europeans.

The former occupations of immigrants differed from the occupational distribution of the residents of Israel in 1948. Such a discrepancy necessarily brings about a certain amount of oc-

[12] For a description of Youth Aliyah, see Norman Bentwich, *Jewish Youth Comes Home* (London: Victor Gollancz Ltd., 1944), and Hanoch Reinhold, *Youth Aliyah: Trends and Developments* (Jerusalem: Jewish Agency, Youth Aliyah Department, 1957).

cupational dislocation. Proportionately, more immigrants than old-timers were engaged in commerce, trade, crafts, and industry. Many of the immigrants working in commerce were actually peddlers, whereas such workers among the resident population were more often shopkeepers. In addition, many craftsmen and industrial workers among the immigrants had worked in small workshops, whereas the old-time Israelis in this category included a greater proportion of factory workers. There were no differences between immigrants and old-timers in administrative, clerical, liberal, and technical professions. However, fewer immigrants had been engaged in agriculture. Immigrants who had been engaged in crafts and industry were frequent among the North Africans, compared to the Europeans. In all countries the most frequent specific occupation listed under crafts and industry was the clothing industry. Immigrants from Asia were more numerous in commerce and trade than those from Europe and Africa. Fewer immigrants from Africa and Asia than from Europe had been engaged in the liberal and technical professions.

THE ECONOMIC PICTURE

The War of Independence, through which Israel had just come in 1948, imposed a heavy burden on its economic and social systems.[13] The actual physical destruction brought about by the war put certain land and economic enterprises out of operation and required considerable investment for reconstruction. The financing of the war drained the country of public and private finance. In addition, the widespread conscription took so many men and women out of their regular occupations that a major readjustment of the entire economy was required. The problems of absorbing a mass influx of immigrants came over and above those imposed by the war.

The vast majority of the immigrants who arrived during the period studied came with practically no means whatever. Their

[13] For the background of the economic situation during this period, see *Luach Ha'aretz, 1949–50* (Tel Aviv: Ha'aretz Press, 1950), pp. 77–86; *Government of Israel Year Book, 1949–50, Government . . . , 1950–51,* and *Government of Israel Year Book, 1951–52* (Jerusalem: Government Printer, 1952).

17

general poverty was a function of the facts that they had emigrated from D.P. camps in Europe or countries from which they were not permitted to remove their material possessions (for example, Rumania) or that they had owned very few material goods in their countries of origin (immigrants from North Africa, Yemen, and Turkey).

In order to provide gainful employment for a new immigrant in industry, agriculture, or one of the crafts, it was estimated that £I 1,000 was needed in addition to the sum needed to provide the immigrant with housing. Capital investment of such size was not made quickly available; it took the government some time to organize loans from international sources and from the already heavily taxed local population. There was considerable hope at the time for American investments; however, the soaring prices, which had begun to rise during the Mandate period and continued to after the war, made such investments unattractive. In addition, the unfavorable dollar exchange was felt to be highly unrealistic, causing considerable loss to the foreign investor.

Although agricultural production increased during 1949 and 1950, it was still far from supplying the needs of the growing population. Much of the former Arab land remained uncultivated during this period. Prices of agricultural goods were high. In the vital citrus industry, the high cost of labor, coupled with the inexperience of immigrant workers, resulted in such high prices that the Israeli producers were unable to compete on the world market. The Histadrut [14] objected to the owners' attempts to adjust wages in accordance with the productivity of the individual workers, and the result was that long negotiations over wages caused the growers to miss the season. Many orchards were also abandoned as unprofitable enterprises.

In response to the constantly rising prices, the government introduced an austerity rationing program during the spring of 1949. By April of that year the cost-of-living index (based on 100

[14] For information on the Histadrut (General Federation of Labor), see Janowsky, *op. cit.*, pp. 67–71, and Lehrman, *op. cit.*, pp. 158–178.

in August, 1939) had risen to 371, compared to 337 at the time of the establishment of the state. The threefold function of the austerity program was (1) to lower prices, (2) to save foreign currency by importing a minimum of food and other goods bought with hard currency while ensuring an adequate diet and goods essential to the population, and (3) to increase production, which would be adversely affected by the other two aims, in order to provide more employment and put more goods on the local market. Immediately upon the introduction of the austerity program, prices began a slow but steady decline until August, 1950, when the index reached 321.[15] Strict rationing of goods from abroad or those manufactured locally with imported raw materials was introduced. The supply of food to consumers was lowered to a bare minimum, with one small portion of meat (irregularly distributed) and two eggs a week being standard fare. Almost all essential foodstuffs, candy, clothing, and many other consumer goods were rationed at controlled prices. These prices were kept extremely low and within the reach of all, even the lowest-income groups. The government established the official prices of many goods by cutting into what were believed to be the excess profits of manufacturers.

The severe restrictions of the austerity program imposed many difficulties on the population. Food and consumer goods were in such short supply that housekeeping was physically difficult; shopping was a tedious affair, requiring waiting in line and repeated visits to the shops to obtain the few goods that were available. The rationing system never achieved a very high degree of efficiency insofar as distribution of goods was concerned. Consumers often felt that they were being imposed on by an inefficient, bureaucratic system. This feeling was shared by manufacturers, who rebelled at the distribution methods of wholesale goods as well.

Immigrants, even those in the camps who were not engaged in actual housekeeping, were also hard hit by the rationing pro-

---

[15] After August, 1950, the cost-of-living index began to rise again. To a large extent, this was a local reaction to the Korean war and the instability of world prices which came in its wake.

gram. For many, their first impression of Israel was that of a deprived country in which life was depressing and difficult. Supplies which they were accustomed to having were in short supply or could not be obtained at all. Those who had immigrated from Arab countries were generally used to a Middle Eastern diet and found the European-oriented food-rationing program, in which little choice of foods was possible, a considerable hardship; rice, oil, sugar, and meat were in very short supply, whereas margarine and eggs, which they were less accustomed to using, were distributed to them. The general shortage, coupled with the unmet dietary needs of several segments of the population, resulted in the development of a black market. Added to the general difficulties of their first period in the country, it was difficult for most immigrants to view the rationing program with much perspective.

The austerity program of 1949 and 1950 succeeded in checking what might have been a runaway price increase. It also managed to supply the entire population, regardless of income or status, with the minimum dietary essentials. At the same time, it did not really succeed in solving the more basic economic problems which faced the country: the needs to increase investments, augment local production, provide employment for immigrants. Despite the lowering of prices, the decrease was not sufficient to attract foreign investors to Israel. Nor were local enterprises willing to expand under a system of rationing and strictly controlled wholesale and retail prices. The rationing of imported raw materials and the control of profits practically paralyzed local and foreign investments. Thus unemployment remained widespread, not only among the immigrants still in the transit camps, but also among those who had found more permanent housing in abandoned Arab dwellings.

Housing represented one of the most severe problems faced during this period. A housing shortage existed in the country even before the mass immigration began. This shortage was not felt so much during the first months of immigration, when new arrivals were housed in abandoned Arab homes. In this manner, the first 117,000 arrivals were established in Jaffa, Haifa, Jerusalem, Ramle, Lydda, Acre, Tiberius, Safad, and in several smaller, formerly Arab communities. However when these houses were occupied, the only alternative was for the immigrants to remain in the transit camps until housing could be constructed for them. The extreme shortage of investment capital severely hampered the public building program. During 1949 and 1950, only 30,000 dwelling units were constructed by the government and the Jewish Agency combined. These apartments were of minimum standard, small, and entirely inadequate for the needs of the growing immigrant population. Still, for the few families who were fortunate enough to move into such an apartment, it was a considerable improvement over the transit camp. Private builders contributed little to alleviating the housing shortage; the high costs of building and the controlled rentals resulted in the construction of only so-called luxury cooperative houses which sold at exorbitant prices. Since mortage funds were not readily available, private building could serve only the needs of the highest-income groups.

2 · The Framework

What most typifies the immigrants is the temporary and ambivalent status in which they find themselves. They are between two worlds, the familiar surroundings of their country of origin and their permanent locus of settlement in the Israeli social system. The transit camp suspends them in time and delays their physical and social entry into the stable framework of the new society. In some cases, this delay lasted as long as a year, not so much because of a deliberate policy about settlement, but because of a lack of any other choice in the settlement of the sudden mass of new arrivals.

Insofar as the individual immigrant was concerned, his stay in the transit camp hardly assisted his entry into the new society. He was given very little formal instruction concerning problems he was likely to meet or the appropriate means for resolving them in the local context. Nor was there sufficient informal contact with the established social system to permit much independent learning of the roles and values of the culture. The result was a feeling among the transit camp residents that they were marking time, were getting nowhere, or were suspended in time and space.

This book deals with certain social processes characteristic of the transition period in the immigrant's life, when he is struggling with the uncertainties and ambiguities of the transit camp situation. It is a study of the factors which aid or deter the immigrant as he undergoes the strain inherent in such a situation. I shall investigate some of the problems and social processes which are characteristic of a large group of people suspended in time in an unstructured social situation. Within this context, I shall also observe some of the first steps toward acculturation, bearing in mind that I can observe only the earliest attempts of the immigrant to enter the Isreali social system and that these attempts are made in a temporary and isolated environment insofar as actual entry into the social system is concerned.

THE TRANSIT CAMP

The social atmosphere of the immigrant transit camp may usefully be described as a state of anomie: a lack of norms, structure, and certainty.[1] The immigrant is living at the fringe of Israeli society in an atmosphere that has not absorbed the norms of that society. Neither goals nor means of achieving them are clear in his mind. Other than the general goal of settlement and a permanent job, he may have a far from clear image of how such goals would fit into the context of Israeli culture. Furthermore, if a goal is clearly defined in his mind, it may be inappropriate to the institutional structure of Israeli society; for example, an immigrant who hopes to open a small clothing shop or peddle as he did in his country of origin has a goal which is not entirely sanctioned by the occupational value system of Israeli society. On the other hand, even if appropriate goals were defined

---

[1] Robert K. Merton, *Social Theory and Social Structure* (Glencoe, Ill.: The Free Press, 1949), pp. 125–149.

by the immigrant, he is not likely, in the isolated atmosphere of the transit camp, to be able to determine modes of behavior that will be instrumental to their achievement. Finally, even if he does know what the appropriate institutionalized means are, they may not be available to him. The social isolation of the transit camp makes it difficult for the immigrant to pick up cues that will assist him in defining the appropriate norms of Israel.

Not only are the society's goals and means appropriate to achieving these goals largely unknown to the immigrant in the transit camp, but the values and norms of his country of origin have, to a large extent, been rendered inappropriate in the Israeli situation. This is not a function of his being in the transit camp per se, but rather of his general status as an immigrant who has been uprooted from the traditions of his past. The inappropriateness of former goals may take a variety of forms, depending on the circumstances and the nature of the crisis under which the immigrant left his country of origin (compulsion, as in the case of refugees; voluntarily, as in the case of some immigrants from Western Europe or countries in which they sensed impending dangers). In some cases, there may be a conscious rejection of the norms and values of the former society, which is associated with a complex of unfavorable experiences and attitudes. Such a rejection may well have existed before emigration. In other cases, there may be a carry-over of some of the former norms and values despite a feeling that they are not entirely appropriate in the new context. For, despite the social isolation and lack of real understanding of the new values, there is, nevertheless, likely to be a measure of sensitivity among immigrants to the wide differences between local norms and those to which they may still wish to adhere. In such cases, the result is likely to be something approaching a type of "ritualistic" conformity to the former norms.[2]

Such a situation is conducive to considerable strain for the individual, in addition to the strain inherent in the immigrant

---

[2] *Ibid.*, pp. 140–142.

role. Undoubtedly, the strain is magnified in the transit camp situation; the rejection or inappropriateness of former values is experienced by all immigrants. However, the isolation of the transit camp delays learning new roles, norms, and values, which, in a more settled situation and with greater contact with Israeli society, might be more quickly accepted and might fill the vacuum.

Strain

Strain may express itself in many specific situations and conditions which the immigrant meets during his early period in Israel and the transit camp. First, there is the extent to which his expectations about Israel have been fulfilled by his early experiences in the new society. The expectations are associated with the nature of the information the immigrant received and his ideological commitments before he immigrated. It is important to note here that people who are frustrated with what they find in Israel are functioning under a certain strain. The pressure on the immigrant to formulate plans for his future settlement is also conducive to a certain measure of strain. The fact that the decisions and actual carrying out of such plans can be delayed because of the material support the immigrant is receiving in the transit camp in no way eliminates the need to formulate some plans. This is a real problem-solving situation for the immigrant. The paucity of his knowledge about his new society and its resources, coupled with the pressure to make decisions, is also conducive to strain.

A more specific and prevalent form of strain was induced by the widespread unemployment in the transit camps. The extent to which unemployment actually brings about strain for the individual depends on the extent to which his salient reference groups are similarly unemployed. In a situation of such widespread unemployment that all of the immigrant's friends, acquaintances, and other social reference points are also unemployed, the impact of unemployment may be lessened. At the same time, despite the employment status of the members of one's reference groups, there is little doubt that unemployment itself does act as a general demoralizing factor, especially if it is prolonged.

There appeared to be a feeling among immigrants in the transit camps that they were entitled to a large measure of assistance and support from the public authorities, in particular the Jewish Agency and the government. Such assistance, generally conceived as material and more often specifically financial, was not generally viewed as a favor or indulgence from the authorities, but as an obligation to which the immigrant was rightfully entitled.[3] Needless to say, this was not entirely the view of the authorities who dispensed the aid; there was an attempt to reserve the meager resources for those most in need and to test for eligibility for assistance by family size, employability of the household head, or chronic illness in the family. However, from the immigrant's point of view such tests were generally considered irrelevant, and he was frequently unable to accept as real the shortage of funds and resources, which were extremely limited during this period. Some immigrants did receive assistance of one sort or another in their settlement problems; this assistance ranged from financial aid to advice on appropriate procedures to achieve desired ends (whom to see in government offices, introductions to people of authority). The sources of such assistance were not solely the Jewish Agency and the government, but also friends, relatives, the Army, and various political parties, which were often interested in making political capital of the immigrants. However, despite the apparent proliferation of such sources of assistance, the total resources available were meager, making it impossible to aid most of the immigrants. Failure to receive assistance, when considered in terms of the expectations about assistance, is an important source of strain in the transit

[3] T. Grygier noted this attitude among residents of D.P. camps in Europe after World War II. Some of the respondents had, of course, lived in D.P. camps. It is my impression, however, that this feeling was shared by all immigrants, including the non-Europeans. One possibility, untestable here, is that camp life is conducive to this feeling. See T. Grygier, *Oppression* (London: Routledge and Kegan Paul Ltd., 1954), p. 149.

camp situation. If no one received assistance because of the un-availability of resources, the strain would probably be considerably mitigated. However, the minority which did receive some aid served as a constant source of invidious comparison and a consequent basis for strain for those who were less successful.

The prolonged stay in the transit camp also served as a source of strain to the immigrant. Some of the immigrants in the present study had been living in the transit camps for as long as a year. It is possible that experience with camp life in D.P. camps or concentration camps may have some part in the extent to which this strain is felt by the immigrant. I believe, however, that conditions in the camps were probably so trying that, regardless of similar experiences, they were a basic source of strain to all residents when the stay was unreasonably prolonged.

The types of strain noted here certainly do not exhaust those that could be mentioned. However, they represent the dominant problems faced by all immigrants in the transit camp. These forms of strain are structural parts of the immigrant role and the transit camp situation. In addition to the strain to which the individual is subject by virtue of his status as an immigrant in a transit camp, the types of strain to which any individual is subject and which is intensified by the immigration experience may be mentioned. In this category are such problems as family tension, insecurity, personality difficulties, personal difficulties in employment, and so on.

Response to Strain

The response to strain is one of the dominant themes of this book. Although the transition period is too early to shed much direct light on the adjustment or acculturation problems of the immigrant, the manner in which he responds to the initial strains is highly relevant to his subsequent mode of entry into the new social structure. I am unable in the present context to enter systematically into the latter problem; it is evident, however, that immigrants for whom the strain of transit proved to be too great a trial will be differently oriented to the receiving society from immigrants who successfully weathered the strains.

The first group of chapters will be devoted to the response to the strain of transit. I shall explore certain factors in the immigrant's past and present frames of reference which may be relevant to his response to the strains of transit.

The first factor is a positive one: the immigrant's ideological commitment to Israel and to the values and ends which motivated its establishment. Two chapters will examine the role played by a prior Zionist commitment in the immigrant's response to the strain of transit. One chapter will deal with ideology and decision-making, with particular reference to the problem of making plans for permanent settlement; the other concerns the manner in which ideological commitment conditions the response to the reality of Israel as perceived by the immigrant.

The second factor is a negative one: the role played by the prior experience of a major strain in the individual's mode of response to the present strains of transit. The major strain in the immigrant's earlier experience which I shall study is the Nazi concentration camp experience. How did the trauma of the Nazi concentration camp affect the immigrant's ability to weather the additional, relatively minor, strains of his early period in Israel?

One chapter will examine response to the strain of unemployment. How do various groups in the population respond to the unemployment of the household head? In this connection, I shall consider the role of certain comparative reference groups in mediating between the immigrant's employment status and his morale.

First Gropings at Acculturation

The second major section of the study deals with the immigrant's first gropings to enter the new social system. We have already emphasized the physical and social isolation of the transit camps from the social structure of the Israeli society and the consequent impossibility of carrying through a systematic analysis of acculturation or adjustment to the new society. At the same time, it is of interest to examine the first attempts at entry into the Israeli social system in the isolated environment of the transit

28

camp. Considering the minimum social contact between immigrants and old-timers, what may be said of the immigrant's earliest attempts to approach the new society? Some subjects were in the transit camps for as long as a year, so that it is possible to examine these first attempts over a year-long period. The obvious limitation that the acculturation observed may be quite different from that which is likely to develop in a locus of permanent settlement does not reduce the intrinsic interest in the structure of the early attempts at acculturation.

Orientation toward the Future

The next section projects the immigrant into the future. Two chapters focus on occupational aspirations in an attempt to determine how entry into the Israeli occupational structure is foreseen. Even though immigrants were still in a transitory situation, they were, nevertheless, much concerned with the more permanent problems of ultimate settlement and particularly with their future means of livelihood.

One chapter will deal with the status of the occupations to which immigrants aspire. I shall attempt to locate certain factors which appear to be crucial in determining this status. The other chapter in this section concerns the problem of occupational mobility. Immigration, particularly on so vast a scale, necessarily involves a considerable measure of occupational change. In this chapter I shall investigate certain factors which condition the immigrant to aspire to an occupation which is different from his former job.

Ethnic Reference Group

A theme which runs through the analysis of almost all of the problems mentioned above is the salience of the ethnic reference group for the immigrant during his early period in the new country. I assume that, apart from his immediate family, which in many cases has not been preserved intact in the course of immigration, the most crucial reference group for the immigrant is the ethnic one. This would be especially true in situations where the extended family group is no longer functioning in its traditional manner. The loneliness and isolation to which we have already referred can be somewhat mitigated by reference to the one group which remains fairly stable in an extremely unstable social environment. One would expect the reference role of the ethnic group to be intensified during this period, because of the absence of other meaningful groups to which the individual can refer for information about norms of behavior, values, and attitude formation. The ambiguity of the new social environment, plus the detachment from familiar landmarks, makes such information particularly important. During the early period in Israel, the ethnic group was the only functioning group which could play this role. Needless to say, its information was often inappropriate to local social situations, but it nevertheless performed a major function in providing a stable point of reference for the immigrant.

Many of the most affectively toned attitudes and behavior patterns have their roots in the complex of the ethnic culture. Such patterns concern food habits, child-rearing practices, family relationships. These are among the most tenacious culture traits of immigrants and are least likely to change quickly in a new social environment. The general tenacity of these ethnic patterns provides another basic reason for using the ethnic theme throughout the study. Table 2 presents a picture of the variety and size of ethnic groups which made up the sample population.

The analysis does not use specific ethnic membership, but groups immigrants in two general categories, Europeans and non-Europeans. Although a certain measure of the uniqueness of specific cultural backgrounds is lost in this procedure, it presented other advantages. There were two reasons for this grouping. From a substantive point of view, it would seem that, despite marked differences between specific groups and despite a number of unique cultural characteristics, two common cultural characteristics mark the groups labeled "European" and "non-European." The former are almost all of East European origin and consequently share many of the traditions and culture patterns common to that area. The non-Europeans, although they consist

TABLE 2

ETHNIC GROUPS IN THE POPULATION SAMPLE

Country of origin	Number		
Europeans			
Poland	337		
Rumania	104		
Bulgaria	103		
Hungary	48		
Czechoslovakia	47		
Germany and Austria	33		
Yugoslavia	33		
China *	5		
Other European countries	63		
Total		773	41%
Non-Europeans			
Libya	391		
Turkey	322		
Egypt	186		
Morocco	90		
Tunisia	35		
Iraq †	24		
Algeria	12		
Persia	8		
Syria and Lebanon	7		
Yemen ‡	4		
India	2		
Other non-European countries	11		
Total		1,092	59%
No answer	1		
Total		1,866	100%

* Included among the Europeans because immigrants to Israel from China are culturally of Russian origin.

† The mass immigration from Iraq arrived too late in 1950 to be included in the study (see Chapter 1 and Appendix B).

‡ Circumstances beyond my control prevented the inclusion of the Yemenite immigrant population in the sample (see Chapter 1 and Appendix B).

of North Africans and Middle Easterners, are characterized by the fact that they have all emigrated from Arab-dominated countries; they have been surrounded and influenced by Moslem culture for hundreds of years. The position of the Jews in the Arab countries varied at different periods, ranging from extreme subservience to a fair amount of freedom. But in none of these countries did the Jews enjoy real equality. This tradition of subservience to an intolerant majority population serves as a bond among the groups termed "non-Europeans." In addition, the non-European immigrants as a whole are distinguished from the Europeans by a more widespread and traditional religious orientation; by a stronger emphasis on the extended, rather than the nuclear, family as a social, often a residential, unit; and by a generally lower educational and economic standard.

The technical reason for the grouping of the ethnic groups into Europeans and non-Europeans has to do with the small numbers in some of these groups. Table 2 indicates that many of the ethnic groups do not appear in the sample in numbers sufficient to permit reliable statistical analysis of the sort that uses several breakdowns.

3 · History and Methods

The present study was first planned in the spring and summer of 1949, during the height of the mass immigration to Israel. Certain Israeli government offices, sensing the lack of any descriptive information on the immigrants, their reaction to the country, and the process of their absorption into the new society, proposed a systematic study that would yield as much information as possible on these subjects. It was thought at the time that a study of immigrants in the transit camps would represent only the first stage of such a research undertaking, the plan being to continue with a study of immigrants in their more permanent settlements and a comparative analysis of a population of old-timers. The first and last of these studies were carried out; the second was, unfortunately, never executed, owing to lack of funds. Essentially, therefore, this book represents a report of the first stage of the broader study, focusing on the earliest stage of immigrant adjustment in the transit camps. Whenever they are meaningful, I shall also introduce comparative data from the sample of old-timers.

After a series of articles appeared in the local press describing conditions of immigrant absorption and arousing much public interest and criticism, the authorities became aware of the striking dearth of systematic information on this important subject. Accordingly, the Israel Institute of Applied Social Research was commissioned to design and carry out a comprehensive study. Few formal hypotheses were formulated at the time the study was initiated since the objective was to learn as much as possible about the process of immigrant absorption. A fairly comprehensive questionnaire covering a variety of topics was designed.

THE QUESTIONNAIRE

The questionnaire covered six major topics: occupational problems, social relations in the transit camp, morale, attitude toward the host society, acculturation, and level of information about Israel. Details of the questionnaire, as well as some simple frequency distributions, are presented in Appendix A.

Occupational Problems

The problem of making a living was one that faced all immigrants. Despite the fact that for the time being they were being supported in the transit camps by public funds, the question of settling into an income-producing occupation must constantly have loomed large. The public authorities were, of course, interested in moving immigrants into self-supporting jobs as quickly as possible. At the same time, a certain lack of congruence existed between the over-all goals of the society as viewed by the settlement authorities and the occupational goals of many immigrants. The incongruence is associated, on one hand, with the ideological orientation of the society as well as with its economic structure as viewed by those in authority. Immigrants, on the other hand, because of historic and economic factors, often aspired to very different occupational goals from those desired by the authorities. For example, preference was shown to immigrants who were willing to engage in farming. Similarly, the authorities were reluctant to encourage such traditional Jewish occupations as shopkeeping except for people who were physically unfit for other, more "productive" jobs. The severity of this conflict may be seen from the fact that at the time of the study only 34 per cent of the immigrants expressed any interest in farming whereas 60 per cent expressed a preference for shopkeeping. Furthermore, only 17 per cent reported having heard anything about the information campaign by which the authorities were trying to impress upon immigrants the advantages and benefits offered to those who chose a farming career (see Appendix A).

The period of the study was one of extreme economic strain, during which the social and economic institutions of the newly established state were struggling to absorb a mass influx of immigrants. One of the serious results was widespread unemployment during the first year the immigrant was in Israel: 76 per cent of the men and women interviewed reported themselves unemployed. Clearly the employment problem provoked both economic and psychological strain.

Social Relations

Life in the transit camp was, of necessity, bleak. The physical conditions generally left much to be desired: living conditions were crowded; food at the communal dining halls, although sufficient, was drab; there were few provisions for recreation; there were long waits for every conceivable need. One of the most depressing factors was the widespread unemployment.

What kind of social life developed in such an environment? How was family life affected? What can be said of the structure of interpersonal relations among persons of such widely differing backgrounds who were suddenly thrown together to be neighbors? Was there any real contact with Israeli society through the various media of mass communication, or was the isolation social as well as physical? [1]

---

[1] Bearing in mind the basic differences between a temporary immigrant transit camp and a Japanese relocation center, it is of some interest to compare the attitudes observed by Alexander Leighton in *The Governing of Men* (Princeton: Princeton University Press, 1946).

Morale

In the questionnaire, morale was viewed as a multidimensional variable with no necessary correlation among its component parts. Thus, six aspects of immigrant morale were investigated. For example, "orientation toward the future" attempted to assess the balance of the respondents' optimism or pessimism about their personal future in Israel. "Personal adjustment" probed the over-all feeling of well-being and security. "Disappointment with Israel" dealt with the immigrants' reactions to the reality of the new country as compared to his prior expectations.

Attitude toward Host Society

The questionnaire attempted to gain some insight into the immigrants' first responses to the population and certain institutional structures of the host society. One area attempted to assess the immigrants' perception of friendliness or hostility of the host society. Another concerned attitudes toward the government, in particular its efforts in helping immigrants. In addition, an effort was made to determine the immigrants' major sources of advice and information—namely, whether he generally found these in other immigrants or in members of the Israeli community.

Acculturation

Only the earliest stages of acculturation could be observed during the first year immigrants were in the new society. Indeed, it may be questioned whether the term "acculturation" is appropriate for this period. Nevertheless, an attempt was made to observe certain aspects of the earliest stages of acculturation. The procedure was to observe the extent of conformity to a number of norms and values which were defined as ideal Israeli characteristics. I have assumed that these represent norms and values toward which conformity on the part of immigrants was expected during the period of the study, so that acceptance of them represented an indication of integration into the social system. The norms chosen were deliberately idealistic ones toward which the society had, as it were, taken an official stand. They concern such ideal values of Israeli society as agricultural settlement, free immigration, ethnically mixed housing, and collective as opposed to self-orientation.

Level of Information about Israel

Ronald Taft, in his model for social assimilation of immigrants, has emphasized the importance of knowledge about the new society as the first step in entering the social system.[2] I refer here not so much to knowledge of norms or values of the new society as to information concerning its language, social and political institutions, cultural life, and population structure. The manner in which such information is acquired and assimilated increases our understanding of adaptation to the new society a great deal.

In addition to the six major sections of the questionnaire, a number of background variables were, of course, included.

GATHERING DATA

Planning and design was begun in the spring and summer of 1949, interviewers were recruited and trained in the fall, and the field work took place during the following winter and spring, ending in May, 1950. Analysis was not systematically carried out, however, owing to an unexpected cut in funds. Consequently the Institute was able to carry out only sporadic analyses of very limited parts of the material, little of which was published. The data were never fully analyzed until June, 1956, when I was specially commissioned by UNESCO, under its program of aid to member states, to carry out and prepare for publication a complete analysis of the material. Working closely with the Institute staff, this task was completed during 1956 and 1957.

According to information supplied by the Jewish Agency in the fall of 1949, there were 81,207 immigrants living in thirty-five transit camps. Needless to say, these figures changed from day to day; these data, however, served as the basis of the sampling procedure. Sampling was carried out in two stages. A sample consisting

[2] Ronald Taft, "A Psychological Model for the Study of Social Assimilation," *Human Relations*, X, No. 2 (1957), 141–156.

of fourteen transit camps was drawn, and in each camp a systematic sample of the adult residents was chosen. One thousand eight hundred and sixty-six adults were interviewed (see Appendix B).

Finding interviewers with appropriate training and experience proved difficult. The Institute was fairly new and had not built up a staff of experienced interviewers. The Hebrew University had not resumed its full program of studies after the war, nor was its young social science program able to provide people qualified for the work demanded by the study. There were no other research organizations in the country in which interviewers could have obtained previous training.

There was also the language problem. Most of the immigrants had been in the country for too short a period to know sufficient Hebrew to be interviewed freely and comfortably in that language. In order to maximize rapport and encourage the uninhibited expression of attitudes and opinions, it was decided that subjects would have to be interviewed in their native languages. Once this decision was made, it became clear that the first prerequisite for interviewers would be knowledge of the appropriate languages.

The sixteen interviewers who were finally hired were almost all relatively recent immigrants. With the exception of two who had been in the country for about ten years, the interviewers had all arrived during the past year. Among them they possessed a fluent knowledge of nine languages; almost all knew more than one. They all had secondary educations, but only a few had any university training. None had had any training in the social sciences or in interviewing. Their former occupations included teaching, translating, law, and various white-collar jobs.

I ran a two-week training course in interviewing techniques in August, 1949. A number of basic lectures on psychological aspects of the interviewing process were also included. Each of the participants carried out several model interviews in the presence of the others. In addition, I accompanied each interviewer on a number of sample interviews in the field. As a result of the training course and the experimental field work, three of the interviewers were eliminated, leaving thirteen field workers.

The questionnaire, which had originally been formulated in Hebrew, was translated into nine languages: German, Yiddish, French, Arabic, Bulgarian, Hungarian, Rumanian, Polish, and Ladino, a form of Spanish spoken by Jews from Turkey, Bulgaria, Greece, and several other countries. Insofar as possible, an effort was made to keep the language of the translation colloquial. Since they often knew more than one language, interviewers were generally equipped with two or more written translations of the questionnaire.

The draft questionnaire was pre-tested on 150 immigrants in September, 1949. The meaningfulness of the questions as formulated was carefully noted, and a number of revisions were introduced. The first field experience also brought to our attention a number of items which had been omitted and could then be incorporated into the study. One of the major objects of the pretest was to test the attitude areas for scalability. Since the areas were all hypothesized to form Guttman scales, it was necessary to see whether each area originally proposed actually yielded a single dimension. The areas in the final version of the questionnaire were those that were found to scale satisfactorily. It was also necessary to compare the structure of the scales among the language groups to make certain that cultural variations expressed by differences in language did not disturb the structuring of the scales too much. By and large, the language groups were found to scale similarly (see Appendix A).

The actual interviewing began in October, 1949, and was completed in April, 1950. For each camp, teams were composed of interviewers with a knowledge of the languages spoken by the residents of the camp. When the systematic sample of residents was drawn from the list of residents, the country of origin of the subject was recorded on the interview sheet. Thus it was possible to know as soon as the sample was prepared what the language composition of the team had to be. Some camps had a preponderance of North African immigrants and a minority of Europeans, a situation requiring a team with a majority of interviewers knowing Arabic and French. Two or three teams generally operated simultaneously, the object being to complete each camp as quickly

39

as possible and move to the next. The interviewers were generally housed and fed on the camp premises so that they could work at odd hours of the day or night, whenever residents were available for interviewing. In most of the camps, the authorities were extremely cooperative and, whenever possible, provided a room in which interviewing could take place undisturbed. This was particularly important because in the crowded living quarters it would have been difficult to establish the kind of rapport with the subject that was necessary to obtain complete answers.

The interview lasted an average of two hours and was often divided into two sessions for the convenience of the subject, who often found the prolonged questioning tiring. By and large, the interview served somewhat as a catharsis for the immigrant, who was more than happy to have someone to whom he could pour out his heart. Interviewers were instructed to let respondents talk as freely as they wished in order to establish confidence and rapport, but to try to guide them back to the systematic questions. One result of this procedure was that interviews occasionally lasted several hours, with the interviewer playing more the role of a therapist than a collector of social data. However, there was no escaping such a role under the trying circumstances of the transit camps.

Each team was visited by the writer at least once a week in order to maintain close supervision. I also sat in on a large number of interviews to check the field workers and to gain firsthand insight into the problems being discussed.

BACKGROUND OF THE
IMMIGRANT POPULATION

Our population was not entirely comparable with the total immigrant population which arrived in 1949 and 1950 since the field work did not cover the entire two-year period. Furthermore, some of the immigrants who arrived during these years were no longer, or had never been, transit camp residents. The population in the study depended on which groups arrived during the months the field work was carried out. In this respect there were considerable ethnic variations from month to month. It is, therefore,

not entirely meaningful to compare our sample population with
the statistics provided by Sicron on immigration during 1949 and
1950.[3] In effect, there are no systematic data by which we can examine the adequacy of our sampling procedure.

At the same time, it is interesting to compare certain background characteristics of our sample population with the host
population, the people who were in the country at the time the
state was established. Such a comparison should give a picture of
possible differences between the immigrants in the present study
and the society into which they were moving. The material on the
host population is drawn from the census data of November, 1948.
This was six months after the establishment of the state and therefore includes some of the early immigrants as well as those who
had been in the country in May, 1948. However, this represents
the closest systematic data available for such a comparison. We
shall present comparisons with the old-timer population on ethnic
background, sex, and age.[4] With respect to marital status, education, and length of time in Israel, the descriptive data on the
sample population will be given without comparisons.

After the establishment of the state, the ethnic composition
of the Israeli population had shifted considerably as a result of
the mass immigration. The shift expressed itself in a larger proportional representation of people of non-European origin. Over
half (58 per cent) of the immigrant population studied here was
composed of people of non-European origin. Of the total population in the country in 1948, 65 per cent were foreign born, and
only 15 per cent of them had immigrated from non-European
countries. The latter thus represented less than 10 per cent of the
total population at that time.

The sample immigrant population does not differ from the
old-timers in the proportional distribution of men and women.
Slightly more than half of both groups were men: 54 per cent of
the immigrants and 52 per cent of the old-timers.

The age distribution of the immigrants is also similar to that

[3] Sicron, *op. cit.*
[4] *Ibid.*

of the old-timers. Since the sample of immigrants included only those over eighteen, it was necessary, in order to make the comparison meaningful, to compare the percentage distribution of a comparative adult old-timer population. This was not altogether feasible, since the age intervals used by the census do not entirely correspond to those used in the present study. It is our impression, however, that the only difference between the two groups is in the young adult category: 34 per cent of the immigrants are under thirty, whereas only 28 per cent of the old-timers were under twenty-nine.[5] Whatever the differences, however, they were very small. Twenty-six per cent of the immigrants were between thirty-one and forty, 21 per cent were between forty-one and fifty, and 19 per cent were over fifty.

Seventeen per cent of the immigrant sample was unmarried (bachelors, spinsters, widowers, widows, divorcees). Fifteen per cent was married, but had no children. Thirty-seven per cent had one or two children; 31 per cent had three or more children.

It is difficult to compare years of schooling on a cross-cultural basis because of differences in the quality and the level of schools in various countries. In any case, it is of some interest to note that 8 per cent of the immigrant population had only a religious education (i.e., heder or yeshiva). Nineteen per cent had had no formal education whatever. Eleven per cent attended school for fewer than three years, 44 per cent for three to eight years, and 18 per cent for nine or more years. Of the last mentioned, 5 per cent had attended, but not necessarily completed, a university.

Almost all of the immigrants studied had been in the country a year or less. Half (49 per cent) had been in Israel for six to twelve months, a fifth (20 per cent) for four to six months, a quarter (27 per cent) for fewer than four months. Only 4 per cent had been in Israel for more than a year, and none of these had arrived more than a year and a half before the date of the interview.

---

[5] The age intervals for the old-timers was shorter, ranging from twenty to twenty-nine, whereas that of the immigrants was eighteen to thirty. This difference might in itself explain the difference between the two groups.

Two · Response to Strain

4 · Ideology and Decision-Making

One important factor in the immigrant's past which might play a role in his response to the strain of transit is the ideological commitment with which he came to Israel. In this regard, it is important to consider the unique role played by a Zionist ideological commitment in the process of immigration to Palestine, later to Israel.

The strain on which I shall focus in this chapter is the pressure on all immigrants to come to some decision concerning plans for their eventual permanent settlement. This pressure, operating as it does in a situation characterized by absence of knowledge concerning the country and its institutions, would be likely to generate considerable strain.

ZIONISM

In a general sense, immigration to Israel can best be understood in terms of a broad social and ideological movement which views settlement in Israel and constructive participation in its development as highly valued ends. In this respect, the immigrant movement to Israel is qualitatively different from immigrant movements to other countries. The basic difference has to do with the ideology of the Zionist movement and its system of values which has traditionally emphasized the dominance of collective rather than individual goals. Whereas immigrants to Australia or Canada are generally most concerned with personal economic gain and security, the Zionist immigrant to Israel is ideally normatively oriented to the economic and social advancement of the country and only secondarily to his own welfare. A possible disparity between ideal and actual acceptance of the norms should, of course, be borne in mind.

Conformity to the idealistic norms of the ideological movement changed over time with the vicissitudes of history and the varying types of people immigrating.[1] For many of the immigrants who arrived during the brief span of Zionist settlement in Palestine, the ideological motivation played a fairly important role in structuring their frame of reference to the new social system. Immigrants either brought a collectively oriented frame of reference with them or acquired an awareness of it through contact with the institutions and value system of the society. Collectively oriented goals served as a principal source of motivation for much of the voluntary immigration which took place between the end of the nineteenth century and the establishment of the state in 1948. Among the immigrants who were refugees and forced by situational factors to leave their countries of origin, such collective goals played less of a role, although some had ideological commitments. These commitments may not always have been strong enough to have motivated actual immigration under conditions

---

[1] Halpern, *op. cit.*

of less pressure, but an awareness and acceptance of Zionist values were nevertheless present among many immigrants.

The mass immigration which began in 1949 and with which we are dealing here was composed largely of actual or potential refugees. The former included D.P.'s from Europe and people who were driven out of some of the Arab countries; the latter included Jews whose existence in their countries of origin was so precarious that emigration was virtually a necessity. Thus on an over-all level, the basic motivating force to immigrate was probably not so much an internal, ideological one as an external, situational one. It is probably correct to assume that the push to immigration was greater than the pull of the new society. The political situation prior to 1948 practically precluded any immigration to Palestine, however, forcing the most highly motivated immigrants to enter the country illegally. Some potential immigrants, however, had to wait until 1948, so it is possible that a small number of strongly committed Zionists were among the immigrants studied here.

What is perhaps more important to remember is the relatively active role played by the Zionist movement in many of the countries in which the immigrants originated. Membership and activity in such movements, although sufficient in themselves to motivate actual immigration in only a minority of cases, nevertheless provided many immigrants with a frame of reference predisposed toward Israel and its dominant value system. The people who were associated with the Zionist movement did not necessarily accept the traditional collectively oriented value system as an alternative to an individual value system. In a situation of great external pressure to immigrate, it is difficult to determine how much of the motivation is a function of external, situational factors and how much a function of internal, ideological ones. For purposes of the present analysis, it will be sufficient to assume that association with a Zionist movement provides a heightened awareness and sensitivity to the collective goals of Zionist ideology; the stronger the association, the greater the awareness and sensitivity.

In a more general sense, immigrants to other countries may

also be characterized by a frame of reference more-or-less predisposed to the social system of the countries in which they are settling. Such a frame of reference consists of knowledge and expectations concerning various aspects of the social system into which they are moving. The difference in the case of immigration to Israel lies in the fact that a formal ideology systematized the values and goals of the society in a way that made it fairly clear which immigrants had prior commitments to the values and which did not. It is therefore somewhat easier to examine the role of a predisposing frame of reference in the Israel situation; we would expect, however, a considerable measure of generality to emerge from the present findings.

KNOWLEDGE AND DECISION-MAKING

Despite the fact that all of the immigrants in the study were living at public expense in the transit camps, they were nevertheless faced with the need to make some plans for their more permanent settlement, even though the actual carrying out of such plans might be delayed. Our approach was to view this need as an individual problem-solving situation which creates certain tensions and pressures. The latter are particularly felt in a situation of confusion, lack of knowledge, and uncertainty about the norms and institutions of the receiving society. On one hand, the immigrant is faced with a fairly complicated decision-making problem; on the other, he lacks, to a large extent, the means and facilities—knowledge of the new society, appropriate procedures for finding a job and housing, and language—which are necessary to solve such a problem. Lack of knowledge increases the strain which is inherent in decision-making.

In effect, the gradual acquisition of knowledge about the new society and its institutions and norms of behavior would seem to be a prerequisite for making decisions for more permanent settlement. The immigrant can begin to approach such decisions only after he has obtained certain minimum data concerning the society into which he is moving.

How an ideological commitment affects the process of acquiring knowledge about the new society and how information about the country is used in decision-making will be discussed below.

DEFINITION OF THE VARIABLES

Three variables—"Zionism" (ideological commitment), "information about Israel," and "plans for settlement" (representing decision-making)—were defined as Guttman scales.

Zionism

"Zionism" was defined in terms of membership and extent of active participation in the Zionist movement in the country of origin. This represents an institutional rather than an ideological definition and assumes a high, although not necessarily perfect, correlation between organizational activity and ideological commitment. This indirect procedure was necessitated by the difficulty of obtaining valid replies, in retrospect, to questions concerning ideological commitment before immigration; current normative pressures might have influenced respondents to report such a commitment whether or not it had existed. On the other hand, I thought that open declarations of specific forms of organizational activity would be less likely when the respondent had not been active.[2]

The items by which the "Zionism" scale was defined concerned the respondent's former membership in a formal Zionist group,

[2] In the light of the probable lack of perfect correlation between organization activity and ideological commitment, the assumption is relative rather than absolute. I assumed that active Zionists have a greater ideological commitment than non-Zionists. This conservative assumption was also necessitated by the differences among the types of Zionist groups in the countries of origin—pioneering youth movements, adult organizations with differing political orientations—and by the differing positions occupied by such organizations in the social structure of the societies. In some countries, avowed membership in a Jewish, politically oriented movement carried severe political or social sanctions. In such situations, membership in a Zionist group implied a high level of identification with the Jewish group. Some Zionist movements carried on extensive programs of political education for their members; others consisted largely of paper membership. It would be extremely difficult, if not impossible, to separate these elements now; therefore, I took the conservative course and assumed that active membership in a Zionist group indicates more ideological commitment than non-membership.

extent of participation in the activities of that group, and time spent at an agricultural training farm (*hachshara*). A question on agricultural training prior to immigration was included because it characterized the groups and people having the greatest ideological commitment. Such training generally implied the intention to settle in a collective community (*kibbutz*) in Israel. It was, therefore, used as the most positive item on the scale.

Since there was a large clustering of scale scores in the middle of the continuum, indicating membership but relative inactivity in a Zionist organization, I decided to divide the population into three groups: active Zionists (35 per cent), inactive Zionists (45 per cent), and non-Zionists (20 per cent).[3] There may have been some active anti-Zionists in the non-Zionist group, but I had no way of separating them because the respondent was classed as a non-Zionist on the basis of whether there were any Zionist organizations in his country of origin before he immigrated to Israel.

A closer examination of the distribution of the "Zionism" scale indicates that the total percentages are somewhat misleading, particularly when we consider differences owing to sex and ethnic subgrouping. It appears, for example, that only 22 per cent (846) of the women were active Zionists in their country of origin and that among the non-European women the active Zionists represent only 7 per cent (486). Such an unequal distribution reduces the case base considerably, and certain subgroups were very unreliable (there are only thirty-four non-European active Zionist women). Since Zionism is the major independent variable of the analysis, it was decided to limit the empirical tests to the men in the population, bearing in mind the limitation which this sets on the results.

Information about Israel

"Information about Israel" was determined by a brief test concerning social and political characteristics of local life. The scale items covered such topics as whether the respondent knew

---

[3] $N = 1,843$. A small number of respondents did not reply to the "Zionism" questions. This explains the somewhat smaller case base.

what the principal spoken language of the country is, who makes the laws, what happens to people who are openly anti-government, which political parties were currently in the government (the check list included a number of fictional parties), what the overall policy on the East-West question was.

The information scale was cut as close to the median as the scores would permit, and the total population was thereby divided into "better informed" (54 per cent) and "less informed" (46 per cent). There was no meaningful basis for an intensity score on this scale, for items were marked "correct" or "incorrect." The division into "less informed" and "better informed" was, therefore, somewhat arbitrary. Contrasted to the other scales, where intensity curves provided meaningful divisions into "positive" and "negative," this scale must be viewed in a relative sense (see Appendix A).

The men, on whom the present analysis is based, were somewhat better informed than the women in the population; 61 per cent of them are "better informed," and 39 per cent "less informed." It is also of some interest to note that Europeans (regardless of their formal education) are markedly "better informed" than non-Europeans; 78 per cent of the Europeans, contrasted to 37 per cent of the non-Europeans, are "better informed."

Plans for Settlement

The questions on "plans for settlement" focused on the extent to which the immigrant had formulated a clear-cut program for more permanent settlement. In this scale, I was not concerned with what these plans were, but with whether the respondent had made any such plans. The scale might be more aptly termed a scale of "decisiveness of plans for the future," for I was interested in the response to the strain of decision-making judged by whether the immigrant overcame some of that strain by coming to some fairly definite decisions (see Appendix A for items).

How crucial this attitude area was for immigrants is shown by a comparison of the attitudes of immigrants and non-immigrants. In a 1949 study by the Israel Institute of Applied Social Research, soldiers about to be discharged from the Army were asked the same set of questions concerning plans for the future. It was found that 90 per cent (2,246) had definite plans concerning what they would do after discharge.[4] In order to make the comparison of the immigrant population with the Army population meaningful, the immigrant men under forty were separated, and their attitude concerning plans for settlement observed. Only 58 per cent (538) of the young male immigrants had definite future plans; the same percentage is found if we consider only the male immigrants under thirty-five (395). Although I do not have comparative data for the remainder of the population, it would be reasonable to assume that newly arrived immigrants as a whole are markedly more indecisive concerning their future plans than non-immigrants are. Indeed, among immigrant men observed, only 49 per cent (469) of them indicated definite plans for the future.

The instrumental nature of the items in the "plans-for-settlement" scale makes them particularly appropriate for men. Finding housing and a job is traditionally the domain of men in practically all cultures. Although women were also asked these questions, it is reasonable to assume that the questions have a different meaning for them and would be less appropriate for analysis in the same context. In effect, 35 per cent of the women, contrasted to 54 per cent of the men, had definite plans for the future. I therefore limited the empirical analysis to the men in the population. Before proceeding, it is interesting to note that non-Europeans as a whole had fewer definite plans for the future. Only 39 per cent of the non-Europeans, compared with 55 per cent of the Europeans, indicated that they had definite plans for the future. The higher the level of education attained, the more likely the immigrant was to have formulated definite plans; this factor, however, operates independently of ethnic background.

---

[4] The structure of the scale in this study was different from the one in the present study, and the zero point was differently located. Despite this, it is meaningful to compare the proportions in the two populations on either side of the zero point. See Samuel A. Stouffer *et al., Measurement and Prediction* (Princeton: Princeton University Press, 1950), and the mimeographed report of the Israel Institute of Applied Social Research, "Tochniot Chayalim Le'achar Hamilchama" ("Post-War Plans of Soldiers") September, 1949.

RESULTS

Was there any difference between Zionists and non-Zionists in the process of absorbing knowledge about the new society? Did a person's ideological background make a difference in this process?

In order to answer these questions, we observed the level of information attained by immigrants of differing Zionist backgrounds who had been in Israel for varying lengths of time. Table 3 presents these data.

TABLE 3

PERCENTAGE OF "BETTER INFORMED"

AMONG IMMIGRANTS OF DIFFERING ZIONIST

BACKGROUNDS AND LENGTHS OF TIME IN ISRAEL *

Zionist background	Fewer than six months in Israel		More than six months in Israel	
	Percentage			
Active Zionists	41	(174)	64	(251)
Inactive Zionists	23	(212)	36	(191)
Non-Zionists	21	(95)	17	(75)
	$\chi^2 = 18.3$		$\chi^2 = 65.1$	
	D.F. = 2		D.F. = 2	
	P < .001		P < .001	

* The data in this table and all subsequent tables in this chapter are limited to the men in the population.

Table 3 indicates that Zionist immigrants are more receptive to information about Israel than non-Zionist immigrants. Although the percentage of "better informed" increases over time from 41 to 64 among the active Zionists (a difference of 23 per cent), the difference among the inactive Zionists is only 13 per cent, and among the non-Zionists it does not increase at all. The negative difference of 4 per cent is insignificant, and we viewed it as a zero difference. This configuration suggests that gaining information over a period of time about the country depends on the ideological frame of reference from which the new situation is approached. There is no basis for assuming that exposure to opportunities was different for Zionist and non-Zionist immigrants. It is likely that immigrants with a meaningful predisposed frame of reference might actively seek out media of information. Perhaps more important is the fact that with equal exposure, immigrants with a background of Zionism were able to understand information which apparently did not fit into a meaningful frame of reference for the non-Zionists.

Another point of some interest emerges from Table 3. In observing the percentages of "better informed" among those who were in Israel for fewer than six months, I noted that the Zionists' level of information soon after their arrival in the country was considerably higher than that of the non-Zionists. Thus, active Zionists, on arrival in the country, were better informed about Israel and its institutions. But, considering the variables in Table 3 among groups of differing educational background (Table 4), we observed that the initial level of information was affected by Zionism only among the less educated. Among the better educated, the percentage of "better informed" did not depend on Zionist background; all of the better educated, regardless of their Zionist background in the country of origin, showed the same level of information during the early period in Israel.

Table 4 also confirms the findings of Table 3 that immigrants with a Zionist background were more receptive to information about Israel than non-Zionist immigrants. Among the less educated and among the better educated, we found the difference between those who had been in the country fewer than six months and those who had been in the country more than six months was greater among the active Zionists than among the non-Zionists. Among the better educated, the non-Zionists showed a decrease in information over time; however, the number of cases on which these findings are based was too small to be reliable.

In summary, with a given exposure, immigrants with a prior Zionist commitment absorbed more information about Israel, its customs, and its way of life than immigrants without a Zionist frame of reference. This was true regardless of differences in the amount of information with which Zionist and non-Zionist immigrants arrived in Israel. The information to which we refer is the sort that is absorbed in the course of daily living, not as the result of an information campaign. One explanation for this find-

TABLE 4

PERCENTAGE OF "BETTER INFORMED" RELATED TO
ZIONIST BACKGROUND, LENGTH OF TIME IN ISRAEL,
AND EDUCATION

	Fewer than six months in Israel		More than six months in Israel	
	Percentage			
Fewer than seven years of school				
Active Zionists	31	(99)	52	(121)
Inactive Zionists	13	(158)	22	(136)
Non-Zionists	11	(73)	10	(60)
	$\chi^2 = 16.7$		$\chi^2 = 42.3$	
	D.F. $= 2$		D.F. $= 2$	
	P $< .001$		P $< .001$	
More than seven years of school				
Active Zionist	55	(75)	75	(130)
Inactive Zionists	54	(54)	69	(55)
Non-Zionists	54	(22)	47	(15)
			$\chi^2 = 5.56$	
			D.F. $= 2$	
			$.10 > P > .05$	

ing is the selectivity of perception in terms of the perceiver's needs and predisposed frame of reference. The Zionist immigrant, because of his greater understanding and appreciation of the norms of Israel and particularly because of his comprehensive picture of the society and the ends toward which it is striving, was likely to be more receptive to information he met in the course of his daily activities. The non-Zionist immigrant, lacking such an over-all picture of the society, its ends, and values, was less able to fit disparate information into a meaningful framework and thus was less likely to perceive such information. Even if he did perceive it, he was less likely to remember it because he lacked a meaningful framework.

The other question concerned the role of an ideological back-ground in the immigrant's decision-making, specifically about his plans for more permanent settlement. This question will be con-sidered with the previous one, for getting information was viewed as an intermediate step in decision-making. Does information about the new country help or hinder immigrants with differing Zionist commitments to make decisions for more permanent settle-ment? Table 5, showing the extent of decisiveness about plans for settlement among Zionist and non-Zionist immigrants with differ-ing levels of information about Israel, provides the first empirical answer to the question.

TABLE 5

PLANS FOR SETTLEMENT, RELATED TO ZIONIST
BACKGROUND AND LEVEL OF INFORMATION

| Level of information | Ambiguous about the future | | |
	Active Zionists	Inactive Zionists	Non-Zionists
	Percentage		
Less informed	57 (92)	55 (154)	51 (64)
Better informed	34 (322)	44 (218)	59 (76)
	$\chi^2 = 15.4$	$\chi^2 = 4.51$	
	D.F. = 1	D.F. = 1	
	P < .001	.05 > P > .02	

Table 5 indicates that increased information reduces ambi-guity considerably among active Zionists and somewhat among inactive Zionists; more information, however, increases ambiguity among non-Zionists. The reversal is striking and, at first glance, surprising. It seems that when immigrants with a Zionist frame of reference acquire additional information about Israel and its institutions, they put the knowledge to use in formulating decisive plans for settlement; when immigrants without a Zionist frame of reference acquire additional information about the country, however, they are apparently unable to relate it functionally to the major problem which confronts them—plans for settlement—and hence it only increases their confusion. At first, I would not have predicted such a situation, for, on a common-sense level, I would assume that information about the country would play a positive, functional role in helping all immigrants to reach decisions. The same generally consistent picture can be seen in subgroups of varying ethnic origin, although the differences are not always large enough to be significant.

If the same relationship is observed among groups with varying educational backgrounds, the picture is equally consistent, although the differences are not all significant. Table 6 shows that increased education strengthens the original relationship, whereas less education tends to attenuate it. One way of observing this is to note the size of the differences between the percentages of those with less and those with more information in each of the educational groups. The differences between the percentages are consistently greater in the originally observed direction for the group with a higher level of education. This means that a frame of reference with which information can be functionally categorized is particularly useful to people with more education. Such people are apparently more accustomed to having and using information; when information does not find its place in a meaningful frame of reference, they become particularly confused and disoriented.

THEORETICAL CONSIDERATIONS
The empirical findings fall into the framework of certain fairly well-established theoretical formulations. Despite my surprise at some of the findings (notably the dysfunctional role of information for non-Zionists), they are rather meaningful when

considered in a broader theoretical framework. It is my feeling that these serendipitous findings broaden understanding of such processes, so that in similar situations I could predict more accurately.

TABLE 6

PLANS FOR SETTLEMENT, RELATED TO ZIONIST
BACKGROUND, LEVEL OF INFORMATION,
AND EDUCATIONAL BACKGROUND

| | Ambiguous about the future | | |
	Active Zionists	Inactive Zionists	Non-Zionists
	Percentage		
Fewer than seven years of school			
Less informed	48 (62)	55 (132)	53 (55)
Better informed	36 (148)	51 (132)	60 (52)
Difference between percentages	.12	.04	.07
More than seven years of school			
Less informed	72 (30)	59 (34)	44 (9)
Better informed	32 (174)	34 (86)	58 (24)
Difference between percentages	.40	.15	.14
	$\chi^2 = 11.82$	$\chi^2 = 6.31$	
	D.F. $= 1$	D.F. $= 1$	
	P $< .001$	$.02 > P > .01$	

The processes I have observed in this chapter seem to fall in the traditional realm of perception theory, in particular those aspects of it which deal with the role of attitudes, beliefs, and predisposing sets in structuring a person's cognitive world. These concepts are more or less what David Krech and Richard S. Crutchfield call "functional factors" and what Jerome S. Bruner and Cecile G. Goodman call "behavioral" determinants of perception.[5] Muzafer Sherif has emphasized that perception is almost never a purely cognitive, intellectual affair; it is generally highly charged with motivational components.[6] There is ample evidence that people select from the environment according to their needs and predisposing frame of reference. Looking at this situation from a somewhat different point of view, F.C. Bartlett, in discussing determinants of memory, has pointed out the relevance of meaningfulness in that process.[7]

The role of a predisposing frame of reference in structuring perception is of particular importance in ambiguous or unstructured situations. Bruner and Goodman have noted that, generally speaking, the world as seen by most people is highly "equivocal," thus calling on a large number of behavioral factors to condition perception.[8] Sherif has stated that "the effect of social factors coming from without (suggestion, group pressure, etc.) and of internal factors (motivation, attitudes, etc.) increases with vagueness, 'indeterminateness,' and decreases with the clarity and structuredness of the stimulus situation." [9]

It seems that immigrants, because of their status as newcomers in an unfamiliar social system, face a particularly ambiguous set of social stimuli. Cues which evoke a clear-cut response from those familiar with the culture and its institutions meet with uncertainty from immigrants, who are unable to interpret or categorize them. The decision-making problem itself involves information about many unknown aspects of the Israeli social system and thus pre-

[5] David Krech and Richard S. Crutchfield, *Theory and Problems of Social Psychology* (New York: McGraw-Hill Book Company, Inc., 1948), pp. 81–84, and Jerome S. Bruner and Cecile G. Goodman, "Value and Need as Organizing Factors in Perception," *Journal of Abnormal and Social Psychology,* XLII (1947), pp. 33–44. For a summary of theory in this area, see also Floyd H. Allport, *Theories of Perception and the Concept of Structure* (New York: John Wiley & Sons, 1955), chap. 13.

[6] Muzafer Sherif, *An Outline of Social Psychology* (New York: Harper & Brothers, 1948), particularly pp. 66–75.

[7] F.C. Bartlett, *Remembering* (Cambridge, England: Cambridge University Press, 1932).

[8] Bruner and Goodman, *op. cit.,* p. 36.

[9] Sherif, *op. cit.,* p. 227.

sents the immigrant with an ambiguous set of stimuli. There are many questions which cannot be adequately answered in the crowded, bureaucratically run transit camp.

In this theoretical framework, the difference between acquisition of information by Zionists and non-Zionists becomes more meaningful. An ideological orientation which provides an over-all frame of reference about the new society for the immigrant results in selective perception on his part, so that data which may be meaningless to the non-Zionist immigrant are fitted into a meaningful cognitive framework by the Zionist. In this manner, the fact that during their first year in the country Zionists increase their information whereas non-Zionists do not can be explained.

The second problem discussed comes under the rubric of cognitive organization and concerns the instrumental role of such organization for a person. Bruner, J.J. Goodnow, and G.A. Austin have pointed out that perception always involves an act of categorization. One of the achievements of such categorizing is the "direction it provides for instrumental activity." [10] This is to say that categorizing indicates certain actions to be appropriate or inappropriate in a given situation. An additional achievement of categorizing which seems relevant here concerns the opportunity it provides for "ordering and relating classes of events." [11]

The categories by which people classify their perceptions reflect not only the language and culture which they bring to the situation, but also the frame of reference which characterizes their approach to a given problem. People with one frame of reference would categorize a given phenomenon in such a way as to make it instrumental to a certain end, whereas people with differing frames of reference would categorize the same phenomenon in a way that might be instrumental to another end and possibly dysfunctional for the first.

An example will clarify the role of a predisposing frame of reference in a person's cognitive organization. An immigrant with a Zionist frame of reference might categorize the rather stringent

[10] Jerome S. Bruner, J.J. Goodnow, and G.A. Austin, *A Study of Thinking* (New York: John Wiley & Sons, 1956), p. 12.

[11] *Ibid.*, p. 13.

rationing of meat which he found in Israel as one of the necessary hardships of absorbing large numbers of immigrants and as a means toward stabilizing the economy. An immigrant without a Zionist frame of reference might categorize the rationing as a means of depriving him of his necessary and accustomed food. In the first case, such a categorization would probably be positively functional in assisting the immigrant to identify with the values of the new society; in the second case, such categorizing is not functional in furthering identification with collective ends, but it may provide a framework for rationalizing personal hardship, thus serving a functional role in the immigrant's personal adjustment. The Zionist immigrant relates rationing to a broader category of phenomena, "hardships inherent in building a new country," whereas the non-Zionist immigrant classifies the rationing as "difficulties imposed on me because I am an immigrant."

A somewhat different, but related, way of looking at the same process has been noted by Krech and Crutchfield, who term it "differentiation and isolation of the cognitive field." [12] This is a problem of the relative broadness or narrowness of the cognitive organization, of the extent to which a person isolates the perceived phenomenon from the rest of the field or sees it in its relationships with other phenomena. Problem-solving will be more effective, according to these authors, when the problem is viewed in its broader aspects and attention is paid to the larger sets of relationships which may play a role in solution.

Thus, the second empirical finding may best be understood by considering the role of a predisposing frame of reference in providing for a functional or dysfunctional organization of the cognitive field for problem-solving. The findings relate to the use to which information is put by immigrants with a Zionist or non-Zionist frame of reference. The use to which I refer is problem-solving by assisting the immigrant to formulate plans for more permanent settlement. At first glance, one would expect the immigrant to use relevant information about the country in making decisions and plans concerning his future settlement. It appears,

---

[12] Krech and Crutchfield, *op. cit.*, pp. 135–141.

however, that such use of information depends very much on whether the immigrant is a Zionist. Immigrants with a Zionist frame of reference make constructive use of acquired information; for non-Zionist immigrants, such information is not functional and increases uncertainty rather than decisiveness. This apparently stems from the fact that the Zionist is more likely to classify his information in categories which are relevant to the problem he is facing. In addition, the Zionist is likely to see the broader implications of any information he acquires, whereas the non-Zionist will tend to isolate his information.

The relation of the empirical finding to the theoretical formulation becomes clearer through an analogy with an everyday situation. Think of two people putting together a jigsaw puzzle. One knows in advance what the completed picture is supposed to look like; the other does not. Gradually each picks up more pieces. The first sees the picture increasingly clearly as he picks up the pieces, for he is acquiring more information. The second finds himself growing more confused as he accumulates pieces. This analogy must be qualified by the fact that the second man becomes more confused only until he suddenly sees or guesses what the completed picture is. At that point, pieces begin to fall into place. Presumably, after the non-Zionist has been in the country long enough to acquire some understanding of the general problems of Israeli society, additional information will play a functional role in assisting him to formulate plans. However, at the early stage of settlement with which we are dealing here, this turning point has probably not been reached. The non-Zionists still do not see what the puzzle is supposed to look like, so that additional information only confuses them.

CONCLUSIONS

A note on the limitations of the findings in this chapter is in order. It will be recalled that for technical reasons the data were limited to the men in the population. I would predict the same relationships for women; however, this requires additional study. In addition, the findings are limited in their implications to a brief period of time. I would not predict, for example, that people without a Zionist background would always be characterized by a lower level of information than people with a Zionist background in their country of origin. It would certainly seem reasonable to assume that a time will come when the levels of information would tend to equalize; however, it is impossible with the data at my disposal to suggest at what time this leveling off would occur. With respect to the finding about the functional use of information, it may likewise be suggested that the role of Zionism as a predisposing frame of reference might also be attenuated over time. Again, I am unable to test this assumption systematically.

Nevertheless, I believe that the implications of the present findings are important on the theoretical and the applied levels. On the theoretical level, I am dealing with a problem of perception and cognition, carrying it from the actual selection and organization of stimuli to the functional role of the perceived data in problem-solving. On the applied level, this analysis should provide considerable insight into the effectiveness of information campaigns for educating immigrants, particularly immigrants with varying frames of reference.

5 · Ideology and Frustration

Pursuing the question of the role of an ideological commitment, I shall attempt to determine the extent to which Zionists and non-Zionists were disappointed with Israel as they found it. Does the ideology assist immigrants in this area?

The reality of Israel during this period was one that was likely to evoke frustration. Unemployment was widespread; permanent housing was difficult to obtain. A considerable measure of foresight and stamina would be needed to see beyond the daily difficulties of the immediate situation. It is in this context that a Zionist ideological background assumed a particular importance.

It would be expected that previous identification with the Zionist movement would create certain expectations concerning Israel; these expectations might differ from the expectations of people who had been ideologically uncommitted before immigration. Different expectations would, of course, lead to different responses to the same situation. Looking one step ahead to the possible repercussions of disappointment with Israel, it might be suggested that immigrants with a Zionist commitment would react differently to disappointment with their first experiences in the country than would immigrants without such a background. Again, this reaction is a function of the expectations which the immigrant brought with him as well as of the role played by the ideology itself in insulating or oversensitizing him to situations which deviate from his expectations about the goals of the ideology.

Two basic problems will be dealt with in this chapter: first, the role of the ideology in conditioning disappointment with Israel and, second, some of the repercussions of disappointment with Israel in terms of the immigrant's emotional stability and the possible displacement of such frustration to other behavioral or attitudinal areas.

POSSIBLE RESPONSES

Despite the positive role of the ideology in information-getting and decision-making, we are nevertheless somewhat uncertain about the expectations concerning Israel which would characterize immigrants with an ideological commitment. Knowledge of the specific kinds of norms which were internalized by members of Zionist movements in their countries of origin is incomplete, because the Zionist movements in the countries of origin were structurally so different from each other that even detailed knowledge of each—which is lacking—would make precarious any generalizations about expectations.

Because of knowledge acquired in the Zionist movement, one possible characteristic of people with a prior ideological commitment would be more realistic expectations concerning the country. In such a case, one would expect less frustration with the reality of Israel. This possibility includes an assumption that affiliated Zionists were likely to acquire more correct and applicable information about Israel prior to their immigration because of their exposure to information campaigns and contact with representatives of the Israeli Zionist movement.

Another possibility, which takes the opposite point of view, is that affiliated Zionists are characterized by less realistic expectations concerning the country owing to the exaggerated hopes instilled in them by representatives of the Zionist movement. Here the assumption is that the information imparted by the Zionist movement painted a basically unrealistic picture of Israel by portraying the country as a Utopia, "a land of milk and honey," where all problems would be solved. Thus, although affiliated Zionists may have acquired a greater quantity of knowledge about Israel, the information might have been unrealistic, reinforcing their initial frustration. The relative lack of information of the unaffiliated might have been, on the whole, more realistically oriented to the problems and experiences to be met in Israel.

Similarly, one can speculate about the repercussions of disappointment and frustration with Israel. On the one hand, Zionists who are disappointed might, because of their exaggerated expectations, be bitter and resentful. The disappointment might be a major affective experience to people who had nurtured hopes and dreams of life in Israel. Conceivably they might even show signs of tension or psychological disturbance. On the other hand, the ideological commitment might serve as insulation against frustration, protecting the committed from the emotional disturbance that might otherwise follow such frustration. In this case, the ideology would serve as a source of security and stability in the face of the new experiences which the immigrant meets during his period of adjustment to the new country. From this point of view, the affiliated Zionist, despite his frustration with Israel, would still view the country with relative equanimity and optimism and would not be likely to experience a serious emotional upheaval as a result of his disappointment.

IDEOLOGY AND DISAPPOINTMENT

A Zionist is here defined in terms of the respondent's affiliation and activity in the Zionist movement in his country of origin. The findings are limited to the men in the population.

The first question concerns the role of a Zionist ideological background in the immigrant's disappointment with Israel. Are

individuals with an ideological background more or less likely
to be frustrated by the reality of Israel? At first glance, there appear to be no differences between Zionists and non-Zionists in
their disappointment with Israel. Regardless of Zionist affiliation,
about one third of the population expresses disappointment. (See
Appendix A for items defining "disappointment with Israel.")
However, a closer look at the picture in terms of ethnic background shows a somewhat different configuration. Table 7 indicates two differences. First, Europeans are more disappointed
with Israel than non-Europeans. Second, among the Europeans,
active Zionists are less disappointed with Israel than non-Zionists.
Among the non-Europeans, frustration does not seem to be a
function of Zionism; the percentage disappointed is consistently
smaller than among the Europeans, but there are no real differences among Zionists and non-Zionists.

TABLE 7

DISAPPOINTMENT WITH ISRAEL AS A FUNCTION OF
ZIONIST BACKGROUND AND ETHNIC ORIGIN

	Percentage indicating disappointment with Israel	
	Europeans	Non-Europeans
Active Zionists	37 (265)	30
Inactive Zionists	47 (113)	33
Non-Zionists	63 (30)	28

$\chi^2 = 6.01$
D.F. $= 2$
$.05 > P > .02$

The first finding, that Europeans are more frustrated with the
country than non-Europeans, would seem to indicate that Europeans had higher expectations about Israel than the non-Europeans. This is probably not so much a question of ideological commitment as of general cultural background. It is probably a phenomenon of relative deprivation. Taken as a whole, the Europeans

came from countries with better socioeconomic conditions than did the non-Europeans; the same situation is, therefore, more frustrating to the Europeans, who implicitly compare it to their former environments than it is to the non-Europeans, for whom the same comparison yields a better verdict for the local situation. I was unable to test this interpretation systematically since there were no available comparative data on the standards of living of the Europeans and non-Europeans before immigration. Nevertheless, it would seem reasonable to explain the phenomenon in the light of what is generally known about the socioeconomic conditions in various countries. This explanation also conforms to the general morale of the ethnic groups to be discussed in Chapter 8.

The second finding, concerning the relative insulation of European Zionists against frustration, appears to be a function of the quality of the ideology internalized by members of this group. For the active European Zionist, the ideology apparently is a source of stability and protection against the possible strain of adjusting to the new society. The difficulties which cause the non-Zionist to react in a frustrated manner do not, to a great extent, affect the non-Zionist or do not serve as a source of frustration. Perhaps the ideology gives him some perspective, so that he is able to view momentary difficulties from a larger context which is rewarding. It is of some interest to note that the insulating function of the ideology operates independently of the cultural factor observed in Table 7: all Europeans, regardless of their ideological commitment, are more disappointed with Israel than all non-Europeans; however, among the Europeans, the active Zionists are the least disappointed. But, despite the insulation provided by the ideology, even the active European Zionists show a higher level of frustration than the non-Europeans. For the non-Europeans, the ideology does not seem to play any observable role in their disappointment with Israel; active Zionists do not behave in a different manner from non-Zionists. This suggests that the Zionist movement had no real function for the non-European, at least in the problem discussed here.

The accuracy and usefulness of the information an immigrant had gained in his country of origin also are probably associated with the reality of his expectations. Some people arrived in Israel with more information about the country than others, but it seems that few had no information at all. The more correct the information proved to be, the more realistic the expectations of the immigrant. Respondents were asked about the accuracy of the information they had obtained in their countries of origin compared to what they found Israel to be like. Of course, the respondent's present frame of mind did color his answers to these questions. Thus, people who were disappointed with Israel were more likely to report that the information they had before immigrating was incorrect, and people who reported that they had received incorrect information were likely to be disappointed with the country. With the available data, it was impossible to determine which way the relation operated. In this analysis, however, I regarded "accuracy of information" the independent variable and "disappointment with Israel" the dependent variable.

Table 8 indicates that more Europeans than non-Europeans report that the information they had received before immigrating to Israel was incorrect in the light of what they found the country to be like. Having received more incorrect, less useful, and less realistic information than the non-Europeans, it is not surprising that the Europeans indicate greater disappointment with the country.

Another interesting suggestion that emerges from Table 8 is that active Zionists are less likely to have received correct infor-

TABLE 8

ACCURACY OF INFORMATION

Percentage indicating that
they had received accurate information

	Europeans		Non-Europeans	
Active Zionists	49	(265)	58	(161)
Inactive Zionists	42	(113)	59	(291)
Non-Zionists	53	(30)	67	(138)

mation about the country before immigration. This finding is fairly clear among the non-Europeans, and there is a hint that it may also be true among the Europeans, although among the latter the differences are small. Thus, correct and useful information may have been more available outside the Zionist movement than inside it, or, viewed conversely, the information provided inside the organized Zionist movement was less realistic and useful. In any case, these seem to be the opinions that former members of Zionist organizations report here.

How does the fact that the individual had received correct or incorrect information affect his disappointment with Israel? How is the frustration of Zionists and non-Zionists affected by the type of information they received before coming to Israel?

Table 9 suggests that receiving incorrect information before immigration increases the immigrant's disappointment when he finally comes to Israel. By and large, the relation of disappointment and information does not operate differently for people with differing ideological backgrounds: the figures listed in the column at the far right of Table 9 do not sufficiently differ from one another to warrant the assumption that an ideological commitment makes a difference in how the accuracy of information affects disappointment. This means that accuracy of information plays an approximately equal role in causing disappointment among Zionists and non-Zionists.

The European Zionists' insulation against frustration is, apparently, not a result of better advance information about Israel, since active Zionists had less correct information than others (Table 8). Furthermore, this insulation operates for those who had received incorrect information abroad just as well as it does for those who had received correct information (Table 9). It seems to be more a question of the internalized function of the ideology for the individual immigrant, for the accuracy of the information is not necessarily relevant to the way the ideology operates in reinforcing the immigrant's ego structure against experiences which run counter to the expectations instilled by the ideology. From the ideological movement, the active European Zionist seems to have acquired a frame of reference by which he could organize experiences meaningfully and thus reduce the likelihood of frustration.

Table 9 confirms the other finding already reported: the higher level of disappointment with Israel among the Europeans

TABLE 9

DISAPPOINTMENT WITH ISRAEL AS A FUNCTION
OF INFORMATION, ZIONIST BACKGROUND,
AND ETHNIC ORIGIN

	Received correct information		Received incorrect information		
	Percentage				
Europeans					
Active Zionists	18	(131)	67	(132)	$d = .49$
Inactive Zionists	19	(47)	68	(65)	$d = .49$
Non-Zionists	38	(16)	93	(14)	$d = .55$
Non-Europeans					
Active Zionists	12	(93)	55	(67)	$d = .43$
Inactive Zionists	15	(172)	61	(117)	$d = .46$
Non-Zionists	16	(92)	57	(40)	$d = .41$

than the non-Europeans. It also confirms the relatively non-functional role in disappointment with Israel that a Zionist ideological commitment played among the non-Europeans. Although the differences are not statistically significant, there is a marked consistency in the data.

REPERCUSSIONS OF DISAPPOINTMENT
Besides the distribution of disappointment with Israel among Zionists and non-Zionists, I was interested in how disappointment affects immigrants with differing Zionist backgrounds. Eisenstadt notes that in some cases in which former active Zionists have been frustrated in their attempts to enter the new social system, their frustration has led to apathy, lack of social participa-

tion, and general despair.[1] So far "disappointment with Israel" has been the major dependent variable with which I was concerned. Reversing the logic and using "disappointment with Israel" as an independent variable, I shall now observe how it conditions behavior and attitude in terms of several dependent variables among people of differing ideological backgrounds. One of the serious problems in this analysis is the fact that both the independent and dependent variables are attitudinal. It is, therefore, impossible to determine the direction in which conditioning operates. If one of the variables observed is ascribed (as, for example, "Zionist background" is for the purposes of the present study) and used as the independent variable, the direction of the conditioning cannot be ambiguous. When both variables are attitudinal, however, there is no necessary direction to the relation, if any is found. Thus, in reporting that disappointed Zionists show more signs of psychosomatic disturbance than Zionists who are not disappointed, I am not ignoring the fact that it is equally plausible that psychosomatically disturbed Zionists are more likely to be disappointed.

The first area I investigated was the emotional stability of Zionists and non-Zionists who were disappointed with the country. Is there evidence for any real emotional stress or strain when people who have come to Israel with ideological commitments and specific hopes and expectations of a new way of life are disappointed in what they find? Is there reason to believe that such disappointment would have a more disturbing effect on them than on people who had no ideological commitments?

There is one variable in the study—a scale of psychosomatic disturbances [2]—which should shed some light on these questions. Although it did not provide a complete clinical picture of the emotional state of respondents, the U.S. Army found this scale extremely useful as a screening device. It may thus serve as a rough indicator of personal tension in the present context. Table

---

[1] Eisenstadt, *op. cit.*, p. 153.

[2] I used the same quasi-scale of psychosomatic complaints as that used in the U.S. Army studies. See Stouffer *et al.*, *Measurement* . . . , *op. cit.*, and Appendix A.

10 indicates the distribution on the quasi-scale of psychosomatic complaints of the "disappointed" and the "not-disappointed" groups in terms of their Zionist background.

TABLE 10

PSYCHOSOMATIC COMPLAINTS AS A FUNCTION
OF DISAPPOINTMENT WITH ISRAEL AND ZIONIST
BACKGROUND

	Many psycho- somatic complaints	Moderate number of psycho- somatic complaints	Few psycho- somatic complaints		
	P e r c e n t a g e				
Active Zionists					
Not disappointed	8	55	37	(265)	$\chi^2 = 11.44$
					D.F. $= 2$
Disappointed	16	60	24	(159)	P $< .001$
Inactive Zionists					
Not disappointed	7	59	34	(254)	
Disappointed	7	52	41	(149)	
Non-Zionists					
Not disappointed	7	62	31	(113)	
Disappointed	7	58	35	(58)	

Table 10 shows that the real differences in psychosomatic complaints occurred in the two subgroups of active Zionists— those not disappointed and those disappointed with Israel. The "disappointed" group was more disturbed than the "not-disappointed" group: 16 per cent had a high frequency of complaints, compared to 8 per cent among those not disappointed; only 24 per cent had a low frequency of complaints, compared to 37 per cent of those not disappointed. The differences among the sub-groups of inactive Zionists and non-Zionists were too small to have any real meaning. This configuration seems to suggest that, on an

73

emotional level, disappointment with Israel affects only the more ideologically committed immigrants, who apparently have greater expectations and a deeper affective investment in the country. To them, disappointment seems to come as a shock to their emotional systems, possibly because the reality of Israel meant far more to them than it did to those who were less ideologically committed.

Thus, the non-European Zionist is less disappointed with Israel than any of the other Europeans, Zionist or otherwise, but no different from the other non-European non-Zionists. The levels of expectation concerning Israel are apparently more-or-less the same for all non-Europeans, whether or not they had Zionist affiliations; such norms were determined more by ethnic background than by ideological commitment. It seems, however, that expectations had considerable affective implications for the active Zionists among the non-Europeans. This conclusion stems from the fact that the non-European Zionists who were disappointed with Israel show signs of emotional disturbance.

The ideology of the European Zionist is different in one way and similar in another. The ideology has an insulating function, protecting adherents from disappointment with Israel. On the other hand, it evokes a similar affective involvement, so that Europeans who were disappointed with Israel do show signs of emotional strain as a result of the frustration which came in the wake of their disappointment.

A second question about the general repercussions of disappointment concerns the possibility of bitterness in other areas of attitude or behavior, particularly among former Zionists. Bitterness would be an external indication of the frustration which is likely to follow disappointment and therefore might be viewed as a displacement mechanism. Thus, the question is whether the type of frustration brought about by disappointment with Israel results in any displacement of feeling to other areas. Are frustrated Zionists more bitter than other immigrants? Do they vent their frustration in other areas differently from non-Zionists?

The first area we examined was the immigrant's feeling that he was being exploited. Immigrants were asked whether they felt they were exploited because they were new to the country (see Appendix A). An excessive feeling of exploitation was interpreted

74

to imply bitterness on the part of the respondent. Table 11 shows the distribution of this variable in terms of "disappointment with Israel" and Zionist background.

TABLE 11

FEELINGS OF EXPLOITATION,

RELATED TO DISAPPOINTMENT WITH

ISRAEL AND ZIONIST BACKGROUND

| | Feelings of exploitation among respondents | |
	Not disappointed with Israel	Disappointed with Israel
	Percentage	
Active Zionists	24 (268)	61 (159)
Inactive Zionists	26 (255)	56 (149)
Non-Zionists	22 (110)	46 (58)

Although not statistically significant, there is a strong suggestion of a correlation between frustration and the feeling of exploitation. Regardless of their ideological background, people who were disappointed with Israel are generally more likely to feel exploited than people who were not disappointed with Israel. However, the active Zionists who were disappointed are most likely to feel exploited. The result of this combination is that the group showing the greatest feeling of exploitation is the active Zionists who were disappointed with Israel. Thus, there is reason to believe that the frustration of disappointment has a deeper effect on the active Zionists than it does on those who came to Israel with no ideological commitment. The weaker the ideological commitment, the weaker the effect disappointment has. This configuration is equally clear in the behavior of the two major ethnic groups taken separately.

CONCLUSIONS

With respect to the first question, the findings were very different for the two ethnic groups in the population. As a whole, the Europeans are more disappointed with Israel than the non-

Europeans. This fact might be related to two factors—the greater deprivation of the Europeans and the less accurate information which, they report, they had received before immigration.

As far as the role of ideological commitment is concerned, the data show that for European immigrants such commitment provides insulation against disappointment with the reality of Israel. European Zionists are less disappointed with Israel than European non-Zionists. Among the non-Europeans, the ideology did not perform this function. Thus, the ideology of the Europeans apparently provided some sort of frame of reference for experiences in Israel so that it was possible for the European immigrant to balance disappointments against remote and valued goals rather than against immediate frustrations. For the non-European, the ideology apparently did not provide this sort of balance.

The insulating function of the ideology for the European Zionists does not appear to be a function of better information about the country. It is apparently more closely related to the general orientation provided by the ideology. The reports of the active Zionists, both European and non-European, concerning the information they had received about Israel before immigration indicate that it was not so accurate as the information of the non-Zionists. There is some reason to suspect that useful, realistic, and applicable information was more likely to be found outside the organized Zionist movement than within it. In general, receiving incorrect information about the country before immigration increased the likelihood of disappointment with Israel. Realistic information reduced disappointment.

One set of factors that might be helpful in interpreting the observed configuration, particularly with respect to the insulating function of the ideology for European immigrants, concerns the religious-secular balance of the cultures from which the two major ethnic groups emigrated and the roles played by the Zionist movements in the cultures. On the whole, the non-European immigrants came from cultural environments in which traditional religious values provided the over-all orientation within and outside the Jewish subculture. Operating in these cultures, the Zionist movement had to assume a religious character; a politically oriented, secular movement would have had little meaning to most Jews in non-European countries. The result of this situation was that the orientation to Israel provided by the political movement differed very little from the general orientation to the Holy Land provided by the religous culture and its value system which affected almost everyone regardless of formal affiliation with the Zionist movement. Thus, among non-Europeans Zionist affiliation did not make an important difference in orientation to Israel. Among the European immigrants, on the other hand, the stronger secular influences in the Jewish subculture and the broader social system gave the Zionist movement an entirely different meaning. Despite the fact that there were religious people among the European Jews and religious wings in the Zionist movement, the basically secular culture which characterized Europe resulted in a greater difference in commitment and orientation between those affiliated, and those unaffiliated, with the Zionist movement. In a basically secular culture, political affiliation carries more ideological meaning than it does in a traditional religious frame of reference.

The second problem, the repercussions of disappointment among immigrants with and without an ideological background, was investigated for two purposes: (1) to determine whether disappointment has differing effects on the emotional stability of Zionists and non-Zionists and (2) to determine whether people with ideological commitments displace their bitterness or tension to other areas as a result of the frustration that accompanies their disappointment.

In investigating whether disappointment with Israel might have repercussions on the emotional stability of immigrants with prior ideological commitments, a quasi-scale of psychosomatic disturbances was used. The data show that European and non-European Zionists who were disappointed with Israel do reveal certain signs of psychosomatic disturbance. This was taken to imply that the frustration of disappointment came as a greater shock to people with an ideological commitment because of the emotional investment in Israel that commitment involved.

Thus, the following picture emerged: Both Europeans and non-Europeans acquired from their previous ideological commitments an affectively oriented set of expectations about Israel, so that when they met disappointment, they react negatively. But the same ideological commitment serves another function for the Europeans in providing insulation against disappointment. The ideology does not appear to perform this function for the non-Europeans.

The findings concerning displacement of tension by "disappointed" Zionists are somewhat inconsistent. On one hand, disappointed Zionists show a greater tendency to feel exploited because of their recent arrival in the country. However, there is no evidence that family tension, tension with neighbors in the transit camp, or reduced idealism accompanies disappointment among people with ideological commitments. These findings can, therefore, only be inconclusive.

6 · The Nazi Concentration Camp

Association with the Zionist movement generally represented a positive experience for the immigrant. I shall now discuss the effect of the Nazi concentration camps, a negative experience, to see how it affects response to strain. Is the response to current strain affected by the experience of more severe strain? Does such experience increase sensitivity and susceptibility to new strains or does it make it easier to overcome new strain?

Some of the immigrants in our population had undergone the severe—in many cases, traumatic—experience of life in a Nazi concentration camp. Undoubtedly, this experience is an example of the most severe physical and emotional strain.[1] The present study took place about five years after liberation, so that it is possible to examine how persistent the effects of the Nazi concentra-

[1] See David P. Boder, *I Did Not Interview the Dead* (Urbana: University of Illinois Press, 1949).

tion camp were in conditioning survivors in their response to strain. It would be difficult to imagine a person's emerging from a Nazi concentration camp without certain psychological scars. Some of these might be ephemeral; others might be more firmly entrenched in the person's behavior patterns. The persistent scars and their role in conditioning the response to additional strain interest us here.

To date, most of the studies on the aftereffects of life in a Nazi concentration camp have focused on the immediate reactions to the trauma. They have been written by survivors or immediately after liberation in the temporary camps that were set up to accommodate survivors or in D.P. camps in Europe.[2] But five years had elapsed since the liberation of the concentration camps; thus, it was possible to learn whether the findings of the earlier studies represented only immediate reactions to the trauma and to what extent such reactions—or other reactions—persist.

Before proceeding to the analysis of the response to strain, we must consider the simpler problem of how the experience of a major trauma such as life in a Nazi concentration camp would affect a person's morale. Would survivors of the Nazi concentration camps be more optimistic or more pessimistic about the future than a comparable group of people? On a common-sense level, without reference to data, it would seem that a reasonable case could be made for either of these possibilities—an aftereffect of optimism or an aftereffect of pessimism.

It could be argued that survival per se of the Nazi program of destruction, particularly the anti-Semitic variety, would make a person optimistic about his future. Under the circumstances, survival must have seemed largely fortuitous, the result of factors over which the survivor could have had little control. The very unpredictability—apparently a means of heightening confusion and anxiety among inmates—of Nazi policy in administering discipline and rewards served to increase the uncertainty of

[2] Bruno Bettelheim, "Individual and Mass Behavior in Extreme Situations," *Journal of Abnormal and Social Psychology*, xxxviii (1943), 417–452; M. Niremberski, "Psychological Investigation of a Group of Internees at Belsen Camp," *Journal of Mental Science*, xcii (1946), 60–74; Grygier, *op. cit.*

survival. Remaining alive after the majority of one's co-sufferers had perished might give a person the feeling of good fortune and encourage optimism about his future. Such optimism is produced by a fortiori reasoning: if unknown circumstances combined to save me from destruction in a Nazi concentration camp, surely I will be fortunate in Israel, where conditions are immeasurably more favorable. Thus, the good fortune of survival might reinforce survivors' optimism about their future. Such optimism one year after liberation from a Japanese concentration camp is reported by Wolf and Ripley.[3]

It is also possible that the extreme threat and terror would reduce a person's confidence in the rewards which the future is likely to bring him. Regardless of the extent to which survivors are capable of repressing painful memories, a certain residue of pessimism would be likely to remain. The oppressive experiences per se would induce pessimistic expectations about the future. In support of the latter point of view, Grygier has shown that men who survived concentration camps are markedly more pessimistic in their responses to the TAT (Thematic Apperception Test). He explains the failure to obtain similar results from women survivors by the fact that, in some sense, they are a biased group, since women were not selected for internment at random.[4] Bondy also refers to the effects of the concentration camp on survivors' optimism.[5] However, as previously noted, neither of these investigators could report long-term effects, since Bondy's observations were made in a concentration camp and Grygier's study took place in the D.P. camps a year after liberation.

Thus far, I have not introduced the concept of response to current strain. Our major interest, however, is in the effect of this experience of severe strain on a person's ability to weather additional strains. Here again, a consideration of the possible effects

[3] Stewart Wolf and Herbert S. Ripley, "Reactions among Allied Prisoners of War Subjected to Three Years of Imprisonment and Torture by the Japanese," *American Journal of Psychiatry,* civ (1947), 191.

[4] Grygier, *op. cit.,* p. 221.

[5] Curt Bondy, "Problems of Internment Camps," *Journal of Abnormal and Social Psychology,* xxxviii (1943), 461.

leads to two diametrically opposed theories, which I shall refer to as "softening" and "hardening." Both theories can be supported by equally plausible sociological and psychological reasoning, and I shall attempt to determine empirically which of them actually operates.

The essence of the softening theory is that a previous experience of severe strain would reduce a person's ability to resist additional strain. His defenses are weakened; although he managed somehow to survive a series of extreme trials, he is now no longer able to withstand lesser strains. An analogy may be drawn to a person who has been severely ill and who, instead of developing immunity to other diseases, becomes more susceptible to them. On a conscious level, the survivor says to himself, "I have suffered so much in the past that I certainly cannot withstand any more difficulties." It is as though his reserves have been depleted and cannot be replenished. Minor strain thus becomes magnified to such an extent that he perceives it to present insurmountable difficulties. In psychological terms, it would appear that the threshold of his frustration tolerance has been lowered as a result of having been tested too much.

The hardening theory proposes that concentration camp survivors will be less sensitive to new environmental strains. This does not imply the sort of apathy which has been referred to as characteristic of D.P.'s.[6] It suggests that, although people who did not experience life in a Nazi concentration camp would be sensitive to new strain and react to it, concentration camp survivors would be less sensitive to the same strain and, although their reactions might be qualitatively similar, they would be less extreme. This theory does not propose that the trauma immunized survivors to strain, but that it hardened them against it. Such a theory is based on the assumption that continued exposure to extreme forms of threat and punishment causes a person to build up certain defense mechanisms which tend to insulate him from threatening experiences. In a threatening situation, the mechanism may

[6] Niremberski, *op. cit.*, p. 62; Lloyd J. Thompson, "German Concentration Camps: Psychological Aspects of the Camps," in Henry Letheby Tidy, ed., *Inter-Allied Conference on War Medicine (1942–45)* (London: Staples Press, 1947), pp. 466–467; summarized in *Psychological Abstracts*, xxii (1948), 686.

be the distinction between life in the camp and "real" life outside it, a characteristic attitude of new arrivals in a concentration camp.[7] In one case the mechanism took the form of a heightened in-group orientation of a youth group that arrived at the camp together.[8] Investigations have pointed to the apathy, sluggishness of response, and indifference which characterize prisoners of war during their internment.[9] Whatever the form of the mechanism, its purpose was to insulate the person as much as possible from new threats. The hardening theory proposes that a measure of this insulation—it is difficult to estimate just how much—is carried over by concentration camp survivors to later situations of lesser strain in such a manner that, however different the new strains from those experienced in the concentration camp, the survivor will, nevertheless, be less sensitive to strain than would other people.

DESIGN

Two problems will be investigated in this chapter. The first concerns the effect of a major trauma involving severe strain on optimism. The second concerns the effect of a former major trauma on the structure of response to current strain.

With regard to the first problem, the procedure was fairly straightforward. I examined the current level of optimism of concentration camp survivors and compared it with the level of optimism of people who had not been in a Nazi concentration camp. In order to eliminate the possibility of the effects of current strain, we limited, as much as possible, the analysis of the first problem to people who were not currently subject to situational strain. The question as formulated was: How has the experience of the Nazi concentration camp affected the present level of optimism of people not currently subject to situational strain?

The second problem is somewhat more complex in its analysis.

[7] Bettelheim, *op. cit.*, p. 432.

[8] Bondy, *op. cit.*, p. 461.

[9] Robert J. Lifton, "Home by Ship: Reaction Patterns of American Prisoners of War Repatriated from North Korea," *American Journal of Psychiatry*, cx (1954), 732–739; Harvey D. Strassman, Margaret B. Thaler, and Edgar H. Schein, "A Prisoner of War Syndrome: Apathy as a Reaction to Severe Stress," *American Journal of Psychiatry*, cxii (1956), 998–1003.

I first defined four situations of current strain to which members of our population were subject in varying degrees. I then observed the response to these strain situations among concentration camp survivors and a control population of European immigrants. Response was measured by the proportion of optimists and pessimists in the subgroups. On the whole, I expected new strain to reduce the proportion of optimists; generally speaking, people subject to strain should be more pessimistic about the future than those who are not. However, the softening theory proposes that new strain will induce a *greater increase* in pessimism among concentration camp survivors than it will among those who were not subjected to this experience. On the other hand, the hardening theory suggests the converse: that new strain will induce less increase in pessimism among concentration camp survivors than it will among the control population.

In order to test for the operation of these two theories, a model consisting of four populations was devised. The concentration camp survivors and the control population were each divided into two groups, one subject to current strain and one not subject to current strain. Each of the subgroups was then observed for the proportion of optimists. The difference in the proportion of optimists among those subject to strain and those not subject to strain among the concentration camp survivors and the control population indicated whether a process of softening or of hardening was operating. The paradigm, which was repeated four times, once for each type of current strain, is as follows:

PERCENTAGE OF OPTIMISTS		
Concentration camp survivors		
Subject to current strain	P_1	
		$d_1 = P_2 - P_1$
Not subject to current strain	P_2	
Control population		
Subject to current strain	P_3	
		$d_2 = P_4 - P_3$
Not subject to current strain	P_4	

If the softening theory is the appropriate one, d_1 must be larger than d_2 ($d_1 > d_2$): new strain induces a shift from optimism to pessimism in more concentration camp survivors than in the members of the control population. For the hardening theory to be confirmed, d_1 must be smaller than d_2 ($d_1 < d_2$): new strain induces a shift from optimism to pessimism in fewer concentration camp survivors than in the members of the control population.

It is clear that the testing of the two theories was carried out in terms of the differences between differences in proportions. In general, I expected d_1 and d_2 to be positive, since, regardless of the past, new strain would probably induce pessimism. Confirmation of the softening theory required only that $d_2 - d_1$ be negative and significantly greater than zero, whereas confirmation of the hardening theory required that $d_2 - d_1$ be positive and significantly greater than zero.

THE EMPIRICAL VARIABLES

The empirical analysis was limited to the European immigrants. There were 769 respondents of European origin. Of these, 192 reported that they had been in a Nazi concentration camp; 577 stated that they had not. The former served as the experimental population, the latter as the control. Before defining the other variables, it is of some interest to compare the two populations on certain characteristics (Table 12).

Table 12 indicates that the distribution of men and women among concentration camp survivors does not differ from that of the control population; in both groups there are more men than women. With respect to age and education, however, the two populations show certain differences. The concentration camp survivors are better educated and younger than the control population. (I am speaking of the adult immigrant population—those over eighteen.) Little systematic information is available concerning the policy of the Nazis in confining different age groups to concentration camps, although there is reason to believe that by the end of the war Jews were interned in a fairly wholesale manner. I have only incomplete information on the age distribution of the Jewish populations in European countries, so it is difficult to interpret this age differential. Sicron has commented on the near absence of children and youths in Nazi Europe during World War II, either because they were exterminated or because people did not wish to have children during the war.[10] His comparison,

---

TABLE 12

COMPARISON OF CONCENTRATION CAMP SURVIVORS
AND CONTROL POPULATION

	Concentration camp survivors $N = 192$	Control population $N = 577$	
	Percentage		
Sex			
Men	56	53	
Women	44	47	
Age			
Under forty	61	46	$\chi^2 = 12.24$
			D.F. $= 1$
Over forty	39	54	P $< .001$
Education			
Fewer than seven grades	38	47	$\chi^2 = 4.75$
			D.F. $= 1$
More than seven grades	62	53	$.05 > P > .02$

---

however, is of immigrants of European origin with those from Asia and North Africa, rather than of European survivors of Nazi concentration camps and the Europeans who were never in the camps. It is of some interest to note Friedman's opinion that survival in a concentration camp was not a matter of biological fitness, but of chance.[11]

"Orientation toward the future" was defined by a Guttman

---

[10] Sicron, *op. cit.*, p. 70.

[11] Paul Friedman, "Some Aspects of Concentration Camp Psychology," *American Journal of Psychiatry*, cv (1949), 604, note 7.

scale composed of the following questions: Do you think there is a good chance that you will get settled in the near future? Do you think things will improve for you in the coming years? Do you think you will be happy in Israel? Do you think conditions in Israel will improve with time? The population was divided into two groups, "optimists" and "pessimists." Of the European immigrants observed in this chapter, 59 per cent were classified as "optimists" and 41 per cent as "pessimists." (See Appendix A, where percentages refer to the total population.)

The variable termed "orientation toward the future" serves a double function in this chapter. It is first used to examine the general effect of a former major strain on the present optimism of people not subject to current strain. Second, it is used in the examination of the softening and the hardening theories.

CONDITIONS INDUCING STRAIN

Four conditions which induced current strain were selected on the assumption that people subject to these conditions are suffering some tension and deprivation, compared to people not subject to these conditions. The fact that these conditions are part of the transit situation did not prevent distinguishing those who were more subject to strain from those who were less so. The conditions are qualitatively different and hardly related to one another. Except by inference, I did not attempt to distinguish quantitatively or even qualitatively among the different types of strain. Although there might have been reason to expect different reactions to different forms of strain, I did not investigate this problem systematically. The only assumption is that each of the given conditions placed the individual under more strain than people not subject to these conditions were placed. Three of the conditions are attitudinal, and one is situational.

Failure to Receive Assistance
in Settlement

Respondents were asked: Who has helped you in your settlement problems? Possible answers included the Jewish Agency, government authorities, relatives, friends, the Histadrut (labor federation), a *Landsmannschaft*, the Army, and so on. Respondents could give more than one reply and were free to add their own answers. The type of assistance was not specified, thus permitting recipients of any sort of help to give a positive response. People who stated that they had received assistance from no one were considered to be under more strain than people who said they had received help of any kind.

The strain to which people who received no assistance were subject becomes clear in the light of the widespread expectations of assistance. There was a general feeling among immigrants in the camps that they were entitled to material assistance in their settlement problems, so that people who did not get such aid interpreted this failure as a personal deprivation. It is in this sense that failure to receive assistance represents a form of strain for the immigrant.

It should also be noted that during the mass immigration of 1949 and 1950, when public and private bodies of every variety were mobilized to help absorb the newcomers, failure to receive some sort of assistance was likely to induce strain. The situation being what it was, it was extremely difficult for an immigrant to find, without assistance from some public or private group, a job and housing. Forty-two per cent of the European immigrants reported that they had received no assistance in their settlement problems.

Disappointment with Israel

Respondents were presented with the following questions: In comparison to your hopes before immigration, what sort of impression does Israel make on you now? Are you disappointed in what you have seen of Israel? Are conditions more or less difficult than you had been led to expect? Is it more or less difficult to find a job than you expected it would be before you immigrated? The population was divided into two groups: The "disappointed" and the "not disappointed" (see Appendix A). Among the European immigrants, 42 per cent stated that they were generally disappointed with Israel. I assumed that the "disappointed" group was under greater strain than the "not-disappointed" group.

In considering the meaning of "disappointment" in the present context, it should be recalled that immigrants in the transit camps had little chance to experience normal life in Israel, so that "disappointment" should be regarded in terms of the immigrant's initial impression of the country. Also, the questions are formulated in terms of the impression on the immigrant of the reality of Israel as compared to his expectations. Thus, distortion of recall does not act as a disturbant in view of the purpose of this variable —to distinguish between people under relatively great and relatively little strain.

Length of Time in the Immigrant Camp

This is the only situational variable of the four strain variables discussed in this chapter. Conditions in the immigrant transit camp were exceedingly difficult from a physical and a psychological point of view. There were crowding, lack of privacy, no facilities for normal family life. We assumed that the longer an immigrant was in the transit camp, the more he was subject to strain. Compared to the three attitudinal strain variables, this variable appeared to be a fairly objective measure of strain. I made this assumption despite the fact that part of the population had had experience with camp life in concentration camps and D.P. camps in Europe. Nevertheless, the conditions in the transit camps were so trying that I felt justified in assuming that the longer the stay, the greater the strain, even considering similar experience. Indeed, the similarity of the situation in the immigrant camp to previous situations did appear to play a role in structuring response to this form of strain. Seventy-three per cent of the European immigrants had been living in a transit camp for more than five months.

Family Tension

The following questions concerning intrafamily relations, with particular reference to husbands and wives, were presented: Would you say there is more or less tension between you and your wife/husband than there was before you immigrated? Do you find that your wife/husband is more irritable than he/she was before you immigrated? Would you say that your wife/husband is as considerate of your needs and feelings as he was before you immigrated? Do you feel that the difficulties which your family has met in immigration and resettlement have caused you to increase your esteem for your wife/husband?

These questions probe a problem of general strain, but focus on the specific immigration situation with which I am dealing. The items defined a Guttman quasi-scale by means of which the population was divided into three groups. The intensity function was not used to dichotomize this scale because of the shape of the distribution: 392 respondents gave the consistent reply "no difference" to the items defining the scale, 105 were spread on scores indicating that the situation in the family was better than before immigration, and fifty were distributed on scores indicating that family relations were worse than before. Two hundred and twenty-three people did not answer these questions, because the questions on the family were not relevant to them or because they refused. It was decided to trichotomize this variable, using the "no-difference" respondents as the middle group and the two other groups as "no tension" and "tension," respectively. The "tension" group was assumed to be under more strain than the others. A rough continuum of strain among the three groups was also assumed, with the "no-tension" group characterized by the least strain. Nine per cent of the European immigrants reported "tension" in the family.

It is recognized that the instrument used here is not ideal for probing the delicate and complicated question of family relations. The large number of "no answers" on this series of questions supports the possibility that I did not entirely succeed in probing for strain in the family. At the same time, the respondents defined on the scale as subject to family strain were a fortiori characterized by a greater amount of such strain. The very crudeness of the instrument led me to assume that I was operating at the far end of the "tension" continuum, so that, if anything, the relationship observed should be sharpened. This does not change the fact that some respondents who might, by other techniques, be characterized as having intrafamily tension are lost in this type of analysis.

It is of some interest to note the role played by the concentration camp experience in conditioning the perception of the situations here defined as conducive to strain. In view of the fact that three of the four variables were attitudinal, one might expect the concentration camp experience to have affected their structuring. However, the data indicate that, with the exception of a greater sensitivity to family tension, concentration camp survivors do not report themselves under significantly more strain than the control groups. Thus the strain situations (with the exception of family tension) were unrelated to the independent variable—the concentration camp experience.

TABLE 13

EFFECT OF STRAIN ON IMMIGRANTS' LEVEL
OF OPTIMISM

	Percentage of optimists		
No assistance received	42	(320)	$\chi^2 = 48.2$
			D.F. $= 1$
Received assistance	67	(452)	P $< .001$
Disappointed with Israel	44	(322)	$\chi^2 = 52.0$
			D.F. $= 1$
Not disappointed with Israel	70	(447)	P $< .001$
Longer than five months in camp	58	(559)	$\chi^2 = 1.7$
			D.F. $= 1$
Fewer than five months in camp	63	(209)	$.20 > P > .10$
Tension in family	36	(50)	$\chi^2 = 13.0$
Neutral	61	(392)	D.F. $= 2$
No tension in family	65	(104)	$.01 > P > .001$

What of the relationship of the strain variables to the immigrant's optimism or pessimism about his future? The four strain situations were essentially unrelated to one another despite the fact that three of them were attitudinal and might reasonably have been affected by the immigrant's over-all perception of the situation. Thus there is real evidence for the empirical reality of the strain situations. At the same time, it should be noted that a fairly clear relationship does exist between each of the four strain situations and the respondents' optimism (Table 13). Those subject to strain are consistently less optimistic than those not subject to strain. It is crucial, however, to recall that the proposed analysis is not essentially concerned with the simple relation between the strain situations and optimism and pessimism, but rather with the amount of pessimism induced by strain among concentration camp survivors as compared to the control groups. In such a framework, the strong relation between strain and optimism and pessimism does not damage the logic of the argument.

THE EMPIRICAL DATA

First I shall discuss how a major strain such as life in a Nazi concentration camp affected the immigrant's future orientation in terms of his optimism. (This analysis was carried out only among people not subject to current strain.)

Table 14 presents the proportions of optimists among persons who were under relatively little strain. The concentration camp survivors and the control population were compared for each of the four situations. The data show a consistently smaller proportion of optimists among concentration camp survivors than among the control population. The differences are significant for the first three situations. In the last situation, "no tension in family," the number of concentration camp survivors is so small (only nineteen cases) that it is extremely difficult for a significant difference between the proportions to appear. What would seem to be important is the consistent direction of the results. I therefore conclude that the strain of the concentration camp experience tended to induce relative pessimism among survivors even when they are not subjected to new situational strains.

The concentration camp survivors were younger and better educated than the control population, so that age and education might have accounted for the differences found in Table 14. However, controlling on these variables shows the configuration to remain consistent. Concentration camp survivors are less optimistic than the control group. The only exceptions occurred in the "no family-tension" situation in which the number of cases among the concentration camp survivors was too small to permit statistical

TABLE 14

ORIENTATION TOWARD FUTURE OF CONCENTRATION CAMP
SURVIVORS AND CONTROL POPULATION IN SITUATIONS
NOT CONDUCIVE TO STRAIN

Situations not conducive to strain	Percentage of optimists		
Received assistance			
Concentration camp survivors	59	(109)	sigma $_d$ = .05
Control population	76	(343)	d = .17
			t = 3.40
			P < .001
Not disappointed with Israel			
Concentration camp survivors	60	(106)	sigma $_d$ = .05
Control population	73	(341)	d = .13
			t = 2.60
			P = .009
Fewer than five months in immigrant camp			
Concentration camp survivors	47	(62)	sigma $_d$ = .07
Control population	71	(147)	d = .24
			t = 3.44
			P < .001
No tension in family			
Concentration camp population	53	(19)	sigma $_d$ = .09
Control population	67	(85)	d = .14
			t = 1.56
			P = .12

analysis. In general, there seems to be a tendency for younger and better-educated people to be more optimistic than older and less-educated people, although the trend is not entirely consistent.

The second, and major, focus of the analysis concerns the appropriateness of the softening or the hardening theory with respect to the response to additional current strain by people who had lived in a concentration camp. Table 15 presents the response among concentration camp survivors and the control population to a failure to receive any assistance in settlement. The difference between those subject to strain and those not subject to strain is 18 per cent among the concentration camp survivors and 34 per cent in the control group. Such a configuration seems to confirm the hardening theory.

TABLE 15

ORIENTATION TOWARD FUTURE IN RESPONSE TO FAILURE
TO RECEIVE ASSISTANCE IN SETTLEMENT AMONG
CONCENTRATION CAMP SURVIVORS
AND CONTROL POPULATION

	Percentage of optimists		
Concentration camp survivors			
No assistance received	41	(83)	
			$d_1 = .18$
Received assistance	59	(109)	
Control population			
No assistance received	42	(237)	
			$d_2 = .34$
Received assistance	76	(343)	

$$\text{sigma}_{d_1 - d_2} = .083$$
$$t = 1.92$$
$$P = .05$$

Although the differences found in this table tend to confirm the hardening theory, it can be seen that the t based on the standard error of the difference between differences is on the borderline of statistical significance.[12]

[12] In order to obtain statistical significance between differences of relatively small size, the number of cases in each of the four groups would have to be fairly large. I am limited in particular by the fact that there are only 192 concentration camp survivors, who break into small subgroups when divided

Table 16 shows the response to disappointment with Israel in the two populations. Here the difference between those subject to strain and those not subject to strain is not too great: among the concentration camp survivors there is a difference of 20 per

---

TABLE 16

ORIENTATION TOWARD FUTURE IN RESPONSE
TO DISAPPOINTMENT WITH ISRAEL AMONG
CONCENTRATION CAMP SURVIVORS
AND CONTROL POPULATION

	Percentage of optimists		
Concentration camp survivors			
Disappointed with Israel	40	(86)	
			$d_1 = .20$
Not disappointed with Israel	60	(106)	
Control population			
Disappointed with Israel	46	(236)	
			$d_2 = .27$
Not disappointed with Israel	73	(341)	

$$\text{sigma}_{d_1 - d_2} = .083$$
$$t = .84$$
$$P = .40$$

---

cent, and in the control group a difference of 27 per cent. Nevertheless, the direction is again consistent with the hardening theory, even though this test is not significant when viewed alone.

Table 17 presents "orientation toward the future" in response

into those subject to strain and those not subject to strain. Therefore, instead of testing for the significance of each table giving the response to strain, I viewed the different strain situations as rough replications and tested for the significance of their combined *t*. This is possible because the four strain situations were found to be unrelated. Small *t*'s in the following three tables should, therefore, not be viewed as failure to confirm one or the other theory. This technique was suggested to me by Louis Guttman. The procedure is to sum the individual *t*'s and divide by the square root of the number of the *t*'s, thus obtaining the combined *t*, which is tested for significance.

to the strain of a prolonged stay in the immigrant transit camp. Of the four strain situations defined, this is the only situational one. The picture that emerges is somewhat different from the others, although not inconsistent with the hardening theory. Even though a prolonged stay in the immigrant transit camps results in a smaller proportion of optimists among the control population ($d_2 = .12$), among the concentration camp survivors the effect of a longer stay in the transit camp seems to have a reverse effect: the proportion of optimists increases somewhat among those who have been in the immigrant camp for more than five months ($d_1 = -.06$). It is not entirely clear how to interpret this finding, except to say that it is fairly small and in no way

TABLE 17

ORIENTATION TOWARD FUTURE IN RELATION TO
LENGTH OF TIME IN THE IMMIGRANT CAMP
AMONG CONCENTRATION CAMP SURVIVORS
AND CONTROL POPULATION

	Percentage of optimists		
Concentration camp survivors			
More than five months in immigrant camp	53	(130)	
			$d_1 = -.06$
Fewer than five months in immigrant camp	47	(62)	
Control population			
More than five months in immigrant camp	59	(429)	
			$d_2 = .12$
Fewer than five months in immigrant camp	71	(147)	

$$\text{sigma}_{d_1 - d_2} = .089$$
$$t = 2.02$$
$$P = .04$$

negates the hardening hypothesis. It certainly does not lend weight to the softening theory. Apparently, a longer stay in the immigrant camp does not act as a strain for the concentration camp survivors. This configuration could be a result of the fact that of the four strain situations observed, this is the one that most closely resembles the experience of the concentration camp, which we are using as the basic independent variable. This is not to suggest that the immigrant camp was structurally like a concentration camp in more than a superficial sense—barracks, lack of privacy, little possibility of family life, authority exercised by people over whom the individual had little control. It goes without saying that the critical component—oppression—was entirely absent from the immigrant camp; nevertheless, there was enough external similarity to make the concentration camp survivors practically immune to the strain induced by a prolonged stay in the immigrant camp. Why their optimism increased with the length of their stay in the immigrant camp, I cannot say with any certainty, nor is the increase large enough to warrant much concern.

The last type of strain which we shall examine is family tension. We have trichotomized this variable into groups showing tension, neutrality, and no tension. Table 18 presents the response to this form of strain among concentration camp survivors and the control population. The 223 persons who did not reply to this set of questions are not included in this analysis.

Again, the data tend to confirm the hardening theory; the differences, however, are not significant. The size of the subgroups has been greatly reduced in this table by the large proportion of "no answers."

The response to all four strain situations has consistently been in the direction of the hardening theory. We may, therefore, consider them as four replications of a test for the hardening hypothesis. The significance of the total configuration is tested by combining the individual t's.[13] The sum of the four t's is 6.55. Dividing by two (the square root of four) yields a pooled t of 3.23. The probability of obtaining such a t is less than .001. I may

[13] See footnote 12 of this chapter.

therefore conclude that, although several individual tests of the hypothesis were not of themselves significant, the total configuration is significant. The hardening theory may therefore be said to be the appropriate one in the context defined.

TABLE 18

ORIENTATION TOWARD FUTURE IN RELATION TO
FAMILY TENSION AMONG CONCENTRATION CAMP

SURVIVORS AND CONTROL POPULATION

	Percentage of optimists		
Concentration camp survivors			
Tension in family	41	(22)	
Neutral	47	(96)	$d_1 = .07$ *
No tension in family	53	(19)	
Control population			
Tension in family	32	(28)	
Neutral	65	(296)	$d_2 = .33$ †
No tension in family	67	(85)	

$$\text{sigma}_{d_1 - d_2} = .147$$
$$t = 1.77$$
$$P = .07$$

---

* d_1 is computed by comparing the group indicating "tension in the family" with the *combined* "neutral" and "no-tension-in-the-family" groups. Combined, 48 per cent (115) of the last two groups are optimists.

† d_2 is computed by comparing the group indicating "tension in the family" with the *combined* "neutral" and "no-tension-in-the-family" groups. Combined, 65 per cent (381) of the last two groups are optimists.

DISCUSSION

This chapter has demonstrated that the traumatic strain of the concentration camp experience does have certain fairly persistent aftereffects, specifically with reference to survivors' orientation toward the future and their tolerance for additional environmental strain. Whether such aftereffects can be said to continue after a five-year interval is a subject for further research; we cannot predict with any certainty how much, if any, attenuation occurs. The present data have demonstrated that, after a five-year interval, survivors of Nazi concentration camps are less optimistic about the future when not subject to current strain and are "hardened" to certain additional strain situations.

Viewed together, these two findings point to a psychological framework among the concentration camp survivors which is rather different from that of the control population. Under favorable conditions, the concentration camp survivors are characterized by a more pessimistic attitude toward the future. This pessimism is not much lowered by exposure to additional strain. On the other hand, under relatively favorable conditions, people who had not lived in a concentration camp display more optimism about their futures. However, upon exposure to various additional situational strains, their optimism drops more sharply—often close to the level of the concentration camp survivors and, in some cases, below it. In other words, the pessimism of the concentration camp survivors varies very little with favorable or unfavorable conditions; in this sense, they are "rigid." The control population is more "volatile": on the whole, it is more optimistic, but conditions of strain result in a marked shift to pessimism. Thus, the findings indicate a fairly long-term persistence of the apathy and phlegmatism which have been noted to characterize prisoners during their internment.[14] These attitudes apparently become more than an immediate response to the immediate stress to which prisoners are subjected.

There is no evidence whatever for the alternative theories suggested—greater optimism as a result of the concentration camp experience or softening to new experiences of strain. The remarkable degree of consistency in the empirical results points unmistakably to one theory. Thus, as a result of the severe strain of internment by the Nazis, the concentration camp survivors developed a depressed level of expectations; apparently they are not so relieved to be alive that they view the future in a rosy light. On the

[14] Lifton, *op. cit.;* Strassman, Thaler, and Schein, *op. cit.*

contrary, they appear to have suffered so much that they are not entirely convinced that the future can be kind to them.

The strain of the Nazi concentration camp does not seem to have increased sensitivity and susceptibility to additional strain, however. Although the concentration camp survivors are generally more depressed than people who had not been interned by the Nazis, the experience has not undermined their ability to stand additional hardships. The contrary is the case.

One might have expected the hardening theory to operate less or not at all in such an affective situation as family strain. The data, however, do not confirm this expectation. If anything, there is a suggestion of a fairly high level of hardening in this area: the difference in optimism between the concentration camp survivors reporting family tension and those reporting no family tension is only 7 per cent, whereas the difference among the controls is 33 per cent (see Table 18). However, the size of these differences (but not their direction) is largely a function of the cutting point, so that this specific configuration should not be taken too literally. It is the total picture that depicts the situation.

It is interesting to note, however, that the most hardening appears in the immigrant transit camp, the situation which most resembles the concentration camp in its camp-life qualities. The data demonstrate that concentration camp survivors are not at all sensitive to the strain of additional time spent in the immigrant transit camp. However, exploration of the hardening to different types of strain situations remains a subject for additional research. Our findings in this regard can only be suggestive.

Other Research in the Area

Certain findings of other research in this area were subjected to empirical test within the framework of the present analysis. These findings did not form the major focus of the analysis, nor were they fully explored. Nevertheless, it may be of interest to present such evidence in the present context.

Several studies have pointed to the unchangeability of basic traits of personality even in the face of so extreme an experience as internment in a Nazi concentration camp. These studies have indicated that major disturbances in the personality system do not generally occur as a result of the concentration camp or other severe experiences except in cases where there was evidence of some personality disturbance earlier in life.[15]

The present study included a quasi-scale of psychosomatic complaints, consisting of the same set of items as those used by the U.S. Army.[16] For the present purpose it was trichotomized into fairly equal groups, and the concentration camp survivors and control population were compared on this variable. Table 19 indicates that the two populations do not differ in psychosomatic complaints. This evidence, although in itself fairly limited, would tend to bear out the findings of other research on this subject.

TABLE 19

PSYCHOSOMATIC COMPLAINTS OF CONCENTRATION CAMP SURVIVORS AND CONTROL POPULATION

	High frequency of complaints	Medium frequency of complaints	Low frequency of complaints
	Percentage		
Concentration camp survivors	34	42	24 (192)
Control population	32	39	29 (577)

Another finding to which repeated reference has been made concerns the increased mistrust and suspected hostility on the part of the outside world which are said to characterize concentration camp survivors.[17] It is of interest to determine whether this

[15] G. W. Allport, J. S. Bruner, and E. M. Jandorf, "Personality under Social Catastrophe," in Clyde Kluckhohn and Henry A. Murray, eds., *Personality in Nature, Society, and Culture* (New York: Alfred A. Knopf, 1948); Friedman, *op. cit.*, p. 601; Brian H. Kirman, "Mental Disorders in Released Prisoners of War," *Journal of Mental Science*, xcii (1946), 808–813; Niremberski, *op. cit.*, pp. 66–74; Thompson, *op. cit.*

[16] Stouffer, *op. cit.*, pp. 536–538.

[17] Grygier, *op. cit.*, p. 223; H. B. M. Murphy, *Flight and Resettlement* (Paris: UNESCO, 1955), p. 71; Niremberski, *op. cit.*, pp. 62–64; Thompson, *op. cit.*

attitude persists five years later or whether it was an immediate reaction to the concentration camp.

Two sets of questions aimed at exploring this problem were included in the study. The first concerned perception of hostility in the outside world and requested the respondent to state the extent of his agreement with such statements as "There are a lot of thefts in this neighborhood," "People often try to take things from me by force," "You can only get along by strong-arm methods around here," "This neighborhood has a bad influence on children." The second set of questions focused on the immigrant's feeling that he was being exploited, particularly as a result of his status as an immigrant. The respondent stated the extent of his agreement with such statements as "You have to be careful here because people generally give you less than what is really coming to you," "People try to take advantage of us because we're new in the country," "I don't feel that people around here are fair." (See Appendix A.) In Table 20, the concentration camp survivors are compared with the control population on these two attitudes.

TABLE 20

PERCEPTION OF HOSTILITY IN THE OUTSIDE WORLD
AND FEELING OF EXPLOITATION AMONG
CONCENTRATION CAMP SURVIVORS
AND CONTROL POPULATION *

	Percentage perceiving hostility		Percentage feeling exploited	
Concentration camp survivors	41	(192)	33	(192)
Control population	43	(577)	33	(577)

* These variables are based on separate questions.

The lack of differences between the two populations is striking. The only conclusion can be that, five years after liberation, any distrust and perception of hostility found among concentration camp survivors immediately after liberation has disappeared.

It may also be suggested that most of the studies which reported distrust did not include adequate control populations in their research designs.

Finally, it may be recalled that this study, as contrasted to Grygier's, found greater pessimism among both men and women survivors of concentration camps.[18] In his research among D.P.'s, Grygier found pessimism only among men. It should be noted, however, that the populations are not strictly comparable, since the present respondents were all Jews.

[18] Grygier, *op. cit.*

7 · Unemployment and Morale

One of the major sources of strain to which immigrants were subject during their first year in Israel was the extremely widespread unemployment. Undoubtedly, it served as a principal focus of strain for people who hoped to find their place in the social and economic structure of Israel as quickly as possible. This strain would be particularly strong among the men, for whom the occupational role plays an especially crucial function in determining status. For the head of the family, a job acquires a heightened significance in the process of entering the social system. Unemployment, therefore, induces strain not only for the men in the population, but also for their wives and children, who have affective commitments to the head of their family.

Unemployment per se will not induce the same amount of strain in all people. The repercussions of strain are very much a matter of expectations. In this chapter I shall utilize a concept

—the comparative reference group—which plays a role in mediating strain. *The American Soldier* presents considerable data demonstrating that reactions occur and evaluations are made in terms of the individual's comparison of his own situation with those of people with whom, or groups with which, he associates himself.[1] If it is the norm of a salient reference group (e.g., civil servants) to be employed even during a period of widespread unemployment, one would expect lower morale among unemployed civil servants than among unemployed members of groups (e.g., unskilled laborers) in which it is the norm during this period to be unemployed. In both cases we have unemployment; the criteria for responding to it differ, however, in terms of the norms of the comparative reference group.

On a gross level, how does unemployment affect differing groups of immigrants—ethnic groups, age groups, groups differing in the length of time they have been in the country and in their educational attainments? Morale will be defined by a Guttman scale of personal adjustment. The items in this scale are as follows: In general, are you in good spirits? Do you feel worried or confused? Do you think your luck is worse than other people's? Are you sometimes so pessimistic that you feel nothing is worth while? Do you think you'll be able to adjust to conditions in Israel? The population was divided into those with "high morale" (80 per cent) and those with "low morale" (20 per cent). Table 21 indicates how the morale of the subgroups in the population is affected by unemployment.

The morale of immigrants is generally reduced by unemployment, although the differences are sometimes small and insignificant. The major exception are immigrants who have been in Israel for a short time—fewer than six months—and who are not noticeably depressed by unemployment. This picture would seem to fit in with a theory of reduced expectations: very new arrivals apparently do not hope or expect to be employed immediately on arrival; however, with the passage of time, *continued* unemployment

---

[1] Samuel A. Stouffer *et al.*, *The American Soldier* (Princeton: Princeton University Press, 1950), Vol. I.

does reduce their morale. It is less clear why the morale of better-educated immigrants is not affected by unemployment. One possible explanation is the fact that they have a better understanding of the economic difficulties of immigrant absorption and hence are able to view their unemployment as a temporary evil which is a necessity in the early stages of entering a new society.

TABLE 21

MORALE AS A FUNCTION OF UNEMPLOYMENT AMONG
GROUPS DIFFERING IN ETHNIC BACKGROUND, AGE,
LENGTH OF TIME IN ISRAEL, AND EDUCATION

| | Percentage with low morale | |
	Employed	Unemployed
Europeans	22 (162)	29 (248)
Non-Europeans	11 (148)	16 (449)
Under forty	17 (181)	22 (350)
Over forty	16 (122)	19 (345)
In Israel more than six months	17 (234)	27 (287)
In Israel fewer than six months	15 (75)	16 (409)
More than six years of school	22 (135)	24 (218)
Fewer than six years of school	12 (170)	19 (477)

Table 21 also indicates some characteristics of the morale of the different groups. It may be seen, for example, that Europeans are more depressed than non-Europeans (see Chapter 8). Better-educated immigrants are characterized by lower morale than less-educated immigrants. And among the unemployed, the immigrants who have been in the country for more than six months are characterized by lower morale than those who have been in the country for shorter periods. These findings are confirmed when controls are applied. Table 22, for example, shows how employment affects morale among groups simultaneously controlled for ethnic background and length of time in the country.

As noted, one way, although not the only way, to explain the general configuration is in terms of comparative reference groups. If comparative reference groups were functioning in determining an immigrant's morale as a result of his employment status, one would expect to find the highest morale among the people who are employed, but whose comparative reference group is generally unemployed. Conversely, one would expect the lowest morale

---

TABLE 22

MORALE AS A FUNCTION OF UNEMPLOYMENT AMONG
GROUPS DIFFERING IN ETHNIC BACKGROUND
AND LENGTH OF TIME IN ISRAEL

	Percentage with low morale				
	Employed		Unemployed		
Europeans					
In Israel more than six months	22	(142)	35	(130)	$\chi^2 = 6.15$ D.F. $= 1$ .02 $>$ P $>$ .01
In Israel fewer than six months	26	(19)	23	(117)	
Non-Europeans					
In Israel more than six months	11	(92)	20	(156)	
In Israel fewer than six months	11	(56)	14	(291)	

---

among the immigrants who are unemployed, but whose comparative reference group is generally employed. People who more or less conform to the employment norm of their reference group would fall somewhere between the two groups.

Although unemployment was extremely widespread among immigrants during this period, there were certain differences in employment rates of the subgroups of the population. Some people were more employable than others. It may be assumed, therefore, that the subgroups characterized by a high rate of employment would impart higher expectations of employment to their members. Of the European immigrants, for example, 61 per cent were unemployed, compared to 75 per cent of the non-Europeans. Of the respondents under forty, 66 per cent were unemployed; 74 per cent of those over forty were unemployed. Of those in Israel for more than six months, 63 per cent were unemployed, contrasted to 88 per cent of those in the country for fewer than six months. There were also differences among groups with differing educational levels: of those who had completed fewer than six years of school, 74 per cent were unemployed; of those with more schooling, 87 per cent were unemployed.

If one considers the above subgroups as comparative reference groups for their members, he would expect the following configuration of morale: The highest morale should be found among employed non-Europeans, employed older people, employed immigrants who have been in the country for a short time, and employed people with a low level of education. The lowest morale should be found among unemployed Europeans, unemployed younger people, unemployed immigrants who have been in the country for more than six months, and unemployed people with a high level of education.

According to Table 21, this general picture holds. In each of the four fourfold tables comprising Table 21 (e.g., employed and unemployed Europeans and employed and unemployed non-Europeans), the upper right-hand cell shows the lowest morale, whereas the lower left-hand cell indicates the highest morale. In each case, the former represents the group that is unemployed, but whose comparative reference group is generally employed; the latter represents the group that is employed, but whose comparative reference group is generally unemployed. Furthermore, the two cells of the principal diagonal consistently fall between the latter two groups in the level of their morale, although not always in the same order. The groups with intermediate morale represent people whose employment status conforms to the prevalent employment norm of their reference group.

Actually, the differences in the percentages are not always very large. Of interest is the apparent consistency in the pattern. However, in the two middle fourfold tables (Table 21) which show the morale of different age groups and of groups that have been in the country for differing lengths of time, the differences are only of one or two per cent. The most striking patterns emerge from the morale of the two ethnic groups: 29 per cent of the unemployed Europeans show low morale, whereas 11 per cent of the employed non-Europeans indicate such feelings. The remaining two groups fall between these two, with 22 per cent and 16 per cent indicating low morale.

These findings certainly cannot be considered real evidence for the functioning of comparative reference groups. They simply suggest another way of looking at the data. In order to explore the question of reference groups and morale in employment, we shall present some material on ecological reference groups—groups with which the individual is in some spatial contact and to whom he may refer in comparative reference terms.

THE TRANSIT CAMP

The ecological reference group refers to people who, by residence or other factors of physical propinquity, may be included in the individual's salient reference group. The assumption is that physical proximity affords a basis of identification (e.g., "We High Streeters," "We residents of a temporary housing development," or, in the case of immigrants newly arrived in Israel, "We residents of a transit camp"). With reference to employment, such ecological groupings would seem to be particularly salient. Employment opportunities are not randomly distributed over space, but are concentrated differentially—from both a qualitative and a quantitative point of view—in rural-urban locales in accordance with various economic factors. Despite the over-all unemployment which characterized immigrants during the period, there was a differential distribution of employment opportunities in various parts of the country. Thus, one transit camp might be more fortunately located than another.

In view of the likelihood of spatially focused group identifications on the one hand and the differential spatial distribution of employment opportunities on the other, I decided to consider the transit camp as a social group in a reference capacity. Although excessive local identifications could hardly be expected to develop in a situation as trying and as subject to frustration as this one, a certain consciousness of local identification did exist, if only because of fairly prolonged residence in the camp. Furthermore, the norm of available jobs must have been known to most residents, particularly the men. This is not only because of the high salience of employment to immigrant families, but also because the labor exchange in the camps served as an information center, reflecting the day-to-day situation concerning job opportunities in the area. The employment norm was, therefore, known in the camp not only through informal channels of communication, but also through the formal medium of the labor exchange.

The level of employment varied from camp to camp, even though unemployment was widespread. In the fourteen transit camps included in the study, the percentage of unemployed ranged from a low of 22 to a high of 85, although most of the camps were characterized by a fairly high level of unemployment. In dividing the camps into those characterized by a norm of employment and those characterized by a norm of unemployment, I have arbitrarily chosen the 55 per-cent–unemployment level as the dividing point between the two groups. By this definition four camps are characterized as having a norm of employment (55 per cent or less of their populations are unemployed), and ten camps are characterized by a norm of unemployment (56 per cent or more of their population are unemployed). It is clear that the norm we have established is an entirely relative one. The cutting point results in a somewhat lopsided distribution of the camps; however, in view of the economic situation at the time of the study, there would appear to be no other meaningful way to divide the camps in terms of an employment norm.

If the transit camp functions as a comparative reference group, we would expect the following configuration in unemployment and morale: the lowest morale should appear among unemployed people living in camps with a norm of employment, and the highest morale should appear among employed people living in camps with a norm of unemployment. Table 23 presents the empirical data on this configuration.

TABLE 23

MORALE, EMPLOYMENT, AND THE TRANSIT CAMP
AS A COMPARATIVE REFERENCE GROUP

	Percentage with low morale			
	Employed		Unemployed	
Norm of employment in camps	23	(77)	45	(31)
Norm of unemployment in camps	15	(228)	19	(664)

Table 23 confirms the expectations concerning the function of the transit camp in a comparative reference role. The lowest morale appears in the upper right-hand cell among people who live in camps where there are relatively good chances of employment, but who have not succeeded in getting jobs. The highest morale appears in the lower left-hand cell among people who succeed in finding jobs even though they live in camps where the chances for employment are poor. The remaining two groups fall between these in the level of their morale.

Looked at from a slightly different angle, Table 23 also indicates that unemployment generally reduces morale, but particularly that of a person living in a group with relatively good chances for employment. When the group's expectations of employment are low, being unemployed reduces morale, but not very much. A person apparently does not care too much if he is unemployed when everyone else is. One might expect, on the other hand, that those employed when it is the norm to be unemployed would display marked high morale. This was not the case, however. An explanation for this failure might be that the jobs available in a situation of widespread unemployment might be of such low status or remuneration that they do not induce high morale despite the fact that they were hard to obtain.

Another interesting finding emerges from Table 23. Among the immigrants who succeeded in finding employment (the left-hand column), those living in camps with norms of employment are characterized by lower morale than those living in camps with norms of unemployment. This configuration suggests that a norm of employment evokes particularly high expectations about jobs; just any job is not entirely satisfactory. People living in camps with norms of employment seem to have expected better jobs than the ones they got. Although employed, their level of morale is lower than that of the employed groups in camps with norms of unemployment.

SUMMARY

It was found that unemployment generally reduces morale, but not when expectations about a job are particularly low. Thus, the morale of immigrants who have been in Israel for fewer than six months is not affected by not having a job; apparently they do not expect to find one quickly. There is also evidence that the morale of people with a high level of education is not affected by unemployment, possibly because they understand the economic difficulties of the country during this period.

Another way of looking at the same picture was in terms of comparative reference norms. Certain subgroups—Europeans, young people, people in the country for a longer time, and people with a good educational background—are characterized by a higher level of employment. Members of these groups should, therefore, have higher expectations about getting a job, and, if unsuccessful, they should have markedly low morale. On the other hand, people in the other groups—non-Europeans, older people, people in the country for a short time, and people with poor educational background—should, according to this argument, have fewer expectations about their employability. When members of the latter groups do find a job, it should induce particularly high morale. The empirical data generally conformed to this trend, and the configuration was especially marked with respect to ethnic groups.

The question of comparative reference groups, employment,

and morale was further explored using the transit camp setting as an ecological reference group. When the transit camps were divided into those with high employment and those with low employment, it was found that immigrants do refer to the employment norm of the camp in which they are living to set their own level of morale. Highest morale was found among employed immigrants in transit camps with relatively low employment; the lowest morale was found among unemployed immigrants in camps with relatively high rates of employment.

Three · First Gropings at Acculturation

8 · Early Patterns of Acculturation

The tentativeness of the term "gropings" suggests the very early stage of settlement. The temporary nature of the immigrants' settlement status makes it premature to study the entire acculturation process; some irregular and incomplete association with the society did exist, however, and immigrants were undoubtedly feeling their way into it. This chapter will analyze some of the first feelers extended by the new arrivals.

ENTERING A NEW SOCIETY

Entry into Israeli society involves acculturation on the part of the immigrant. He must gradually become acquainted with and adopt the norms, values, and salient reference groups of the new society. Taft has pointed out that this process is no different from that by which people in a society move from one group to another —through army induction, change in social or residential group, social mobility, and so on.[1] In both cases a withdrawal from previous groups and an acceptance of new rights and obligations are involved. The ease of transition largely depends on the differences in the norms and values of the old group and the new group. The phenomenon of mass immigration provides an opportunity to observe this process on a macroscopic level.

The immigrants had been in Israel for a fairly brief time; most of them had arrived less than a year before they were interviewed. From one point of view, it is, therefore, impossible to say much about acculturation because the process has only begun. On the other hand, it is possible to consider changes which occur during the first year spent in the new society, viewing this time span as especially crucial in the immigrant's life because of the impact of new experiences. The latter approach attributes a unique significance to the first year, but does not assume a linear projection of the trends observed.

Acculturation is mediated through various forms of direct and indirect contact with the group into which the individual is moving. At the time of the study, the immigrant population was almost isolated from Israeli life and had little direct contact with the old-timer population. Not only were many of the transit camps located at some distance for the main centers of population, but also transportation facilities were crowded and inadequate. Unemployment was widespread, and, even for the minority who was employed, work did not generally provide the kind of egalitarian relationship with old-timers—most of whom had positions of authority in the job hierarchy—that would foster social intercourse. Language barriers made even well-intentioned attempts difficult. It was during this period that the popular terms "first Israel" and "second Israel" were coined to refer to the relatively privileged old-timers and the isolated, underprivileged immigrants. The use of the terms emphasized the separateness of the two groups.

Despite their physical isolation in the transit camps, immigrants were subject to various forms of indirect contact with the new society through mass media, formal education programs spon-

[1] Taft, *op. cit.*, p. 141.

sored by the government and settlement authorities, Jewish Agency officials who had positions of authority in the camps, and, in some cases, relatives and friends.

Two characteristic patterns of early acculturation emerge, each typifying one of the major ethnic groups in the immigrant population. On one hand, there was a pattern of "approach" to the new society with an attempt to draw close to the new way of life; on the other, there was a pattern of "withdrawal" and what seems to be a rejection of Israeli values and norms and a return to the immigrant society. The "approach" pattern is characteristic of the non-Europeans; "withdrawal" describes the behavior of the European immigrants during their first year in Israel. A variety of data—the mode of gradual acceptance of Israeli norms, the trend of seeking sources of advice and information about the new society, and the general attitude toward the society—consistently points to the patterns.

ACCULTURATION VARIABLES

Acculturation was observed in terms of three variables: (1) acceptance of certain norms which immigrants probably perceived as representative of Israel, (2) seeking immigrants or old-timers as sources of advice and information, and (3) general attitude toward the host population. Each of the variables was observed over a year by dividing the population into groups according to length of time in Israel.

Acceptance of Norms

The immigrant's contact with Israel was largely through formal channels—the mass media, education programs, settlement authorities. Through these channels immigrants were constantly presented with norms to which the society officially expected them to conform. These were not necessarily the norms to which a majority of old-time Israelis would be likely to conform, but rather norms which the society, through its official mediators, presented to the immigrants as representative of Israeli society. These norms are very similar to those presented to youth groups being socialized (acculturated) by official adult or adolescent representatives of

119

the groups and, to a large extent, may be considered representative of the official ideology of the state, especially in its policy for the absorption of immigrants.

It is important to note the distinction between the type of norm being discussed here and the society's actual norms as defined by field research (as discussed, for example, by Alan Richardson [2]). The heterogeneous and somewhat uncrystallized state of Israeli society made the location of widely accepted norms of behavior and attitude difficult. The so-called old-timers were usually immigrants themselves, and they were undergoing a more advanced acculturation. To a large extent, norms were still unique to specific subgroups of the population. From this point of view, the entire question of acculturation is better stated in terms of acculturation to the values of certain subgroups of the old-timer population. The real question is which subgroup the immigrant will choose.

Since contact during the period under observation was largely limited to formal communication media, I focused on the extent of acceptance of certain official norms presented to immigrants through these channels.

The norms chosen for analysis concern four dominant themes of the official Israeli value system. The first relates to the need for a reorientation of the traditional Jewish occupational structure, which, in most of the countries of origin, was largely based on trade, crafts, and, in some cases, professions. This theme grew from a belief in the need for "normalization" of Jewish life in Israel by a redistribution of the traditionally urban population into rural communities as well. More particularly, it expressed itself in a pressure toward rural settlement and manual occupations that had not been characteristic of most Jews in their countries of origin. There was a feeling that immigrants should not settle in the urban centers, but should move into the undeveloped areas. This feeling was accentuated by the need to develop the unsettled portions of the country and by the belief that the cities could not support a mass population influx.

[2] See Alan Richardson, "The Assimilation of British Immigrants in Australia," *Human Relations*, X (1957), 157–165.

The second theme concerned the collective orientation of the ideal value system. This norm expressed itself in a belief that people should be more concerned with collective than individual ends. Rather than seek personal advantage, immigrants should pursue ends that would benefit the society by contributing to the development of the country and its over-all objectives.

The third theme related to "the in-gathering of the exiles" and served as a major *raison d'être* of the new state. It expressed itself in a principle of completely free immigration, despite the economic difficulties of such a policy, for any Jew. The country was considered the traditional homeland of the Jewish people to which any Jew was welcome.

The fourth theme, which is closely related to the third, concerns the equality and non-exclusive status of any ethnic group. All ethnic groups were welcome, desirable, and equal in the new state. During the early period, ethnic differentiation with regard to rights, privileges, or even public recognition of certain cultural characteristics was viewed with disfavor.

With these themes in mind, four specific norms, one for each value, were defined for purposes of analysis. The four norms are "attitude toward urban living," "collective versus individual orientation," "attitude toward free immigration," and "attitude toward ethnically mixed housing." The items defining each attitude scale appear in Appendix A.

Sources of Advice and Information

One indication of entry, or at least a first attempt at entry, into the new society is expressed in a reliance on old-timers rather than other immigrants as sources of advice and information. In seeking appropriate behavior and attitudes, the acculturated immigrant refers to old-time Israelis more often than he does to members of the immigrant group. Needless to say, this process varies with the number of relatives and friends the immigrant has in the old-time population. In the present context, however, a consistent preference for old-timers is viewed as a positive indication of acculturation; a persistent preference for other immigrants as the major source of information and advice is viewed as an impediment to acculturation. A more analytic approach to the question would, of course, inquire into the types of information and advice sought. The procedure here, although subject to certain limitations, does provide an over-all ranking of the immigrants in terms of the group on which they generally relied. The ranking was done by a scale entitled "sources of advice and information—immigrants versus old-timers" (see Appendix A for items defining this scale).

Attitude toward Host Society

In the long run, acculturation probably proceeds despite hostility on the part of the host society. Unconsciously, immigrants accept certain norms and values of the new culture. During the first year, however, the basic orientation of the immigrant to the new society would be a function of his perception of hostility or friendliness on the part of the receiving society. Immigrants who perceive a friendly host population probably respond more favorably to the new society than immigrants who perceive hostility. Thus a scale for "attitude toward host society" was devised with items concerning the immigrant's perception of friendliness or hostility on the part of the host society (see Appendix A for items defining this scale).

ACCULTURATION

In order to examine acculturation over time, the three sets of acculturation variables were observed for change over a year. Ideally, such observation should be conducted by a panel study, but, since the present study provided only one picture of attitudes and behavior, I followed the second-best procedure: to divide the population into groups according to the length of time they had been in Israel and to observe the differential behavior and attitudes of these groups with respect to the acculturation variables. One problem in this type of analysis is the inherent assumption that immigrants arriving at different times during the year do not have differing attitudes upon arrival. The only way that a study of this kind can control this factor is to examine the immigrants for differences in personal background on the assumption that the differences might be related to initial attitudes. The examination showed that more of the immigrants who arrived in the early part of the year were from Europe; the reverse was the case later in the year. Since the analysis is controlled for ethnic origin, the differences it led to are revealed in the presentation.

For purposes of the analysis, the time under consideration was broken into three subperiods. Immigrants were classified into one of the following categories: fewer than four months in Israel (510 immigrants), four to six months in Israel (377 immigrants), and over six months in Israel (975 immigrants). The last category had only 7 per cent (sixty-seven immigrants) who had been in Israel for over a year—but it was only a few months over. The number of Europeans and non-Europeans in each of the subgroups is shown in Table 24.

TABLE 24

LENGTH OF TIME IN ISRAEL

	Europeans	Non-Europeans
	Percentage	
Fewer than four months in Israel	26	74 (510)
Four to six months in Israel	33	67 (377)
Over six months in Israel	53	47 (975)

Table 25 shows that the Europeans' acceptance of the first three norms (although the first is not statistically significant) decreases over time, but that the norm "attitude toward ethnically mixed housing" does not change. Among the non-Europeans, on the other hand, the data show an increase in conformity to the norms "attitude toward free immigration" and "attitude toward ethnically mixed housing," but no change in "attitude toward urban settlement" or "collective versus individual orientation."

It appears that, with respect to *all* of the norms observed, changes in attitude do not occur during the first year the immigrant is in Israel. In cases where some change does occur, however,

123

there is a tendency for the Europeans to conform less and the non-Europeans to conform more.

The second acculturation variable concerns the major source

TABLE 25

ACCEPTANCE OF IDEAL NORMS RELATED TO

TIME AND ETHNICITY

Percentage accepting

	Rural settlement		Collective orientation		Free immigration		Ethnically mixed housing	
Europeans								
Fewer than four months in Israel	34	(128)	52	(127)	79	(130)	62	(130)
Four to six months in Israel	25	(122)	35	(123)	73	(124)	62	(122)
More than six months in Israel	25	(513)	42	(512)	68	(513)	60	(513)

$$\chi^2 = 7.56 \qquad \chi^2 = 6.80$$
$$\text{D.F.} = 2 \qquad \text{D.F.} = 2$$
$$.05 > P > .02 \qquad .05 > P > .02$$

	Rural settlement		Collective orientation		Free immigration		Ethnically mixed housing	
Non-Europeans								
Fewer than four months in Israel	24	(366)	44	(370)	80	(378)	66	(375)
Four to six months in Israel	25	(250)	45	(250)	81	(251)	75	(251)
More than six months in Israel	23	(477)	42	(460)	87	(455)	82	(452)

$$\chi^2 = 8.66 \qquad \chi^2 = 27.67$$
$$\text{D.F.} = 2 \qquad \text{D.F.} = 2$$
$$.01 > P > .001 \qquad P < .001$$

Total population	25	43	78	69

of advice and information. Table 26 indicates a marked difference in the configuration of attitudes of Europeans and non-Europeans; the Europeans' reliance on old-timers decreases during the first year in Israel, whereas the non-Europeans' reliance in-

due to contact with friends and relatives without an[?] ethnic network[?]

Early Patterns of Acculturation

creases. An additional point is the fact that the non-Europeans are consistently more reference-oriented toward old-timers; Europeans depend more on immigrants.

Finally respondents were observed on possible changes in the norm "attitude toward host society." The Europeans display a

TABLE 26

SOURCES OF ADVICE AND INFORMATION RELATED TO
TIME AND ETHNIC BACKGROUND

Preference for old-time Israelis

	Percentage		
Europeans			
Fewer than four months in Israel	64	(127)	$\chi^2 = 15.73$
Four to six months in Israel	60	(123)	D.F. $= 2$
More than six months in Israel	47	(510)	P $< .001$
Non-Europeans			
Fewer than four months in Israel	72	(361)	$\chi^2 = 8.35$
Four to six months in Israel	73	(247)	D.F. $= 2$
More than six months in Israel	80	(447)	$.02 > P > .01$

pattern similar to that already observed (Table 27): a decrease over time in their perception of friendliness on the part of the receiving society. The non-Europeans, on the other hand, show no change in attitude. At the same time, the non-Europeans consistently perceive greater friendliness on the part of the receiving society than do the Europeans.

The picture that emerges from the acculturation variables is not entirely consistent in that over the year there is no change in attitude toward some of the acculturation variables (Tables 25–27). At the same time, a certain over-all pattern can be discerned—a pattern of approach to the society on the part of the non-Europeans and withdrawal on the part of the Europeans. With the exception of the cases in which no change occurs over the year, the data point out the fact that the non-Europeans conform more and attempt to draw closer to the new society (as represented by these norms) than do the Europeans, who withdraw into their own immigrant subsociety. The patterns of approach and withdrawal are further confirmed by the fact that the non-Europeans generally prefer old-timers as sources of advice, whereas the Europeans prefer immigrants. In addition, non-Europeans perceive more friendliness in the receiving society—evidence of a more positive orientation to the society into which they are moving.

TABLE 27

ATTITUDE TOWARD HOST SOCIETY

	Percentage indicating perception of friendliness
Europeans	
Fewer than four months in Israel	69 (127)
Four to six months in Israel	67 (122)
More than six months in Israel	44 (509)
	$x^2 = 35.59$
	D.F. $= 2$
	P $<$ .001
Non-Europeans	
Fewer than four months in Israel	79 (315)
Four to six months in Israel	81 (230)
More than six months in Israel	79 (424)

In sum, the impression from these data is that during the first year in Israel, the non-Europeans are oriented to move into the new society structure on a variety of fronts, whereas the Europeans have, in a sense, insulated themselves and drawn away from the new society.

Acculturation in Australia

A study of British immigrants to Australia provides a number of interesting comparisons with our observations.[3] These are particularly relevant to the pattern of withdrawal observed among the European immigrants.

[3] *Ibid.*

Richardson suggests a first stage of assimilation, which he refers to as "isolation." During this period, the immigrant may resist the new society's norms, and possibly his former beliefs and attitudes are intensified. Richardson explains this behavior by the marginal position of the immigrant, who is physically in one country but emotionally elsewhere. This pattern is characterized by a resistance to change and a certain aloofness from the resident population and its culture and values.

In the case of European immigrants to Israel, the pattern of withdrawal is, in a sense, similar to Richardson's isolation and may result from a certain emotional shock which the reality of Israel and particularly the living conditions in the transit camps brought to these immigrants. It will be seen in the data on realization of expectations concerning Israel that the Europeans are more disappointed than the non-Europeans with the reality of Israel. To the Europeans the bleak conditions of the transit camp and the general difficulties of getting settled in the new country may have come as a considerable shock. Such a shock might well result in the type of withdrawal observed.

In his study of conformity of British immigrants to Australian norms, Richardson found that a tendency to conform began only after immigrants had been in the country for at least seven months; before that there was no change in attitudes toward Australian norms.[4] It is entirely possible that the process of conformity begins among the European immigrants only after seven months—or possibly even more—have elapsed. Our data can give us no hint about the date when the direction of acculturation shifts. Even such a delay, however, does not explain the reduction in conformity among the European immigrants during the first year. Richardson's evidence suggests a future change in the pattern of conformity observed.

At the same time, Richardson does cite other findings similar to ours. These concern the immigrant's feelings of satisfaction with his life in Australia: (1) over-all attitude toward Australia, (2) proportion wishing to return to Britain, and (3) the degree to

---

[4] *Ibid.*, p. 159.

which expectations about Australia had been borne out by the immigrant's experiences. For all three of these attitudes, immigrants showed a decrease in satisfaction with life in Australia during the year of observation.[5] Such evidence fits in well with the pattern of withdrawal noted for Europeans. It also agrees with our findings on morale.

MORALE AND APPROACH
AND WITHDRAWAL

How can we explain the patterns of approach and withdrawal which appear to characterize the two ethnic groups? What factors which might condition these patterns of acculturation can be located?

It would seem reasonable to hypothesize that such a configuration as the withdrawal pattern might be characteristic of immigrants who suffered marked frustration and were particularly depressed by their experiences in the new country; the approach pattern might, with equal plausibility, characterize the immigrants who had met with satisfaction and generally favorable experiences in Israel. What is important in considering the response to experience is, of course, not so much the objective nature of the event, as the immigrant's perception of and reaction to it. Here the cultural background of the respondent, as well as his personality structure, plays a crucial role in determining the nature of his expectations and his threshold of frustration. These are of particular significance in the present analysis, in which all immigrants were subjected to more-or-less similar objective experiences —all were still living in the transit camps, all were facing problems of unemployment and housing, and so on. All did not respond in the same way, however, to the crowding, lack of privacy, bureaucracy, and generally bleak atmosphere of the camp. Nor did all react similarly to the unemployment and seemingly interminable waiting.

What lends further credence to such a hypothesis is the fun-

[5] *Ibid.,* p. 164.

damental difference in the cultural backgrounds of the ethnic groups with which we are dealing. The basic differences would certainly be likely to condition different response patterns to similar experiences. On the whole, the Europeans emigrated from societies with higher standards of living than those from which the non-Europeans came. In general, the Europeans had also had more formal education. The question is essentially one of relative deprivation. On the whole, one would expect the Europeans, with their favorable background, to feel more deprived by the conditions they met in Israel than would the non-Europeans, whose basis of comparison was a less favorable one. Again, this generalization must be qualified by the consideration that some European immigrants were better prepared for the realities of the Israeli situation, whereas some non-Europeans were probably under the illusion that life in the new country would be "milk and honey." However, the evidence indicates that these cases represent a minority. The argument on which the morale hypothesis is based would, therefore, be as follows: the Europeans are more likely than the non-Europeans to feel depressed by their early experiences in Israel because of relative deprivation. In their wake, such depression and lowered morale would bring a certain withdrawal from the new society; more favorable morale would result in a pattern of approach.

Let us first examine the levels of morale of the two ethnic groups. Six morale variables were observed: "orientation toward future," "disappointment with Israel," "personal adjustment," "desire to emigrate," "feeling of exploitation," and "psychosomatic disturbances" (see Appendix A for items defining the six scales). Table 28 presents the morale of the two ethnic groups, and Europeans do show a lower level of morale than non-Europeans on all six variables.

It is also of interest to note the changes which occur in the morale variables over time. How is the morale of the Europeans and the non-Europeans affected by the length of time they have spent in the country? After determining this configuration, we shall proceed to the major focus of interest—how morale affects acculturation.

TABLE 28

MORALE VARIABLES

	Optimistic orientation toward future	Not disappointed with Israel	Positive personal adjustment
	P e r c e n t a g e		
Europeans	59 (766)	58 (766)	83 (770)
Non-Europeans	83 (1,083)	69 (1,079)	93 (1,082)
	$\chi^2 = 131.08$	$\chi^2 = 23.97$	$\chi^2 = 45.12$
	D.F. $= 1$	D.F. $= 1$	D.F. $= 1$
	P $<$ .001	P $<$ .001	P $<$ .001

	No desire to emigrate	No feeling of exploitation	No symptoms of psychosomatic disturbance
	P e r c e n t a g e		
Europeans	79 (767)	67 (756)	28 (766)
Non-Europeans	84 (1,851)	74 (999)	35 (1,854)
	$\chi^2 = 9.39$	$\chi^2 = 10.02$	$\chi^2 = 12.24$
	D.F. $= 1$	D.F. $= 1$	D.F. $= 1$
	P $<$ .001	.01 $>$ P $>$ .001	P $<$ .001

Tables 29 and 30 indicate that the morale of the Europeans does get lower the longer they are in the country. (Only the difference on the norm "orientation toward future" is not significant.) The non-Europeans also show a decrease on two of the morale variables ("disappointment with Israel" and "feeling of exploitation"), but only one can be considered statistically significant. On the remaining three morale variables, the non-Europeans show no change over time. At the same time, it is interesting to note that, even when time is controlled, the previous finding concerning the higher morale of the non-Europeans remains.

These data point to greater feelings of deprivation among the Europeans than among the non-Europeans. Not only are more of the former generally depressed by their early experiences in

Israel, but also their depression grows during their first year in the country. During the first year, the Europeans tend to suffer more from the strain of early adjustment.

At the same time, relative deprivation is only an *intervening*

TABLE 29

ORIENTATION TOWARD FUTURE, DISAPPOINTMENT WITH
ISRAEL, AND PERSONAL ADJUSTMENT, AS RELATED TO
TIME AND ETHNIC BACKGROUND

	Optimistic orientation	Not disappointed with Israel	Positive personal adjustment
	Percentage		
Europeans			
Fewer than four months in Israel	67 (128)	72 (128)	92 (130)
Four to six months in Israel	57 (124)	59 (124)	86 (124)
More than six months in Israel	57 (514)	55 (514)	80 (516)
		$\chi^2 = 11.89$ D.F. $= 2$ .01 $>$ P $>$ .001	$\chi^2 = 11.41$ D.F. $= 2$ .01 $>$ P $>$ .001
Non-Europeans			
Fewer than four months in Israel	84 (377)	72 (375)	95 (376)
Four to six months in Israel	83 (250)	70 (250)	92 (251)
More than six months in Israel	83 (454)	66 (454)	93 (455)

variable in the analysis of acculturation. The crucial question here is not the difference in morale between Europeans and non-Europeans nor the patterning of morale over time. What is of interest is the extent to which the morale variables explain the characteristic ethnic patterns of approach and withdrawal. If these patterns are essentially a function of the different levels of morale of the two ethnic groups, one would expect withdrawal *only* among the Europeans with low morale and approach only among the non-

---

TABLE 30

DESIRE TO EMIGRATE, FEELING OF EXPLOITATION, AND PSYCHOSOMATIC DISTURBANCES, AS RELATED TO TIME AND ETHNIC BACKGROUND

	No desire to emigrate	No feeling of exploitation	No symptoms of psychosomatic disturbance
	Percentage		
Europeans			
Fewer than four months in Israel	87 (128)	85 (128)	98 (128)
Four to six months in Israel	77 (124)	66 (119)	80 (124)
More than six months in Israel	77 (515)	62 (509)	81 (514)
	$\chi^2 = 6.02$ D.F. $= 2$ $.05 > P > .02$	$\chi^2 = 12.70$ D.F. $= 2$ $.01 > P > .001$	$\chi^2 = 22.37$ D.F. $= 2$ $P < .001$
Non-Europeans			
Fewer than four months in Israel	90 (375)	77 (337)	96 (377)
Four to six months in Israel	87 (252)	77 (231)	93 (252)
More than six months in Israel	89 (456)	70 (431)	93 (455)
		$\chi^2 = 6.03$ D.F. $= 2$ $.05 > P > .02$	

Europeans with high morale. Europeans with high morale should, in that case, display either a pattern of positive acculturation or no change. Similarly, the non-Europeans with low morale should display either withdrawal or no change over time.

In order to examine this problem systematically, it is necessary to observe over time acculturation among immigrants with higher morale and immigrants with lower morale. Since we have six morale variables, this procedure must be followed six times on the entire set of acculturation variables. (In order to avoid presenting six large tables, however, I shall present only two.) Table 31 indicates the configuration for one morale variable, "orientation toward future." The other summarizes the total configuration, showing the role of six morale variables in acculturation in a table giving mean percentages. Table 31 is an example of the tables from which Table 32 was composed.

The data in Tables 31 and 32 indicate that differences in morale do play an important role in conditioning approach and withdrawal, but do not explain these patterns as they operate over time. There is a marked tendency for immigrants with higher morale to approach the society more; those with lower morale tend to withdraw from it. At the same time, however, an examination of the data shows that withdrawal often persists even among the Europeans with higher morale although the non-Europeans with low morale frequently display their characteristic approach pattern. The evidence in these tables (and in the five which do not appear here) is not entirely uniform, but there is much consistency.

More particularly, Tables 31 and 32 demonstrate that low morale is always accompanied by less conformity to the norms, less reliance on old-time Israelis as sources of advice, and perception of less friendliness in the receiving society. This trend is seen by observing differences within the two ethnic groups. At the same time, it is clear that morale does not provide a complete explanation of the approach and withdrawal patterns. In Table 31, for example, the Europeans show their characteristic withdrawal pattern even when they are optimistic about five of the six acculturation variables. Only in the norm "attitude toward ethnically mixed housing" does the pattern fail to appear. The same picture appears in summary in Table 32. Thus, with the exception of the norms "attitude toward ethnically mixed housing," the Europeans display fairly consistent withdrawal over time.

The case of the non-Europeans is not too different, for they

TABLE 31

EFFECTS OVER TIME OF ORIENTATION TOWARD FUTURE ON ACCULTURATION VARIABLES

Percentage indicating:

	Acceptance of Norms				Old-timers as major source of advice and information	Perception of friendliness
	Attitude toward urban settlement	Collective versus individual orientation	Attitude toward free immigration	Attitude toward ethnically mixed housing		
Europeans (time in Israel)						
Pessimistic						
Fewer than four months	32	26	71	43	43	62
Four to six months	28	12	68	47	36	52
More than six months	21	23	61	47	33	34
Optimistic						
Fewer than four months	36	65	81	71	74	72
Four to six months	23	53	76	73	79	60
More than six months	28	56	73	70	58	52
Non-Europeans (time in Israel)						
Pessimistic						
Fewer than four months	19	30	66	56	50	49
Four to six months	19	32	57	62	48	55
More than six months	20	31	66	67	68	65
Optimistic						
Fewer than four months	25	47	82	68	76	84
Four to six months	27	47	86	78	78	86
More than six months	24	44	91	85	83	82

TABLE 32

SUMMARY OF EFFECTS OVER TIME OF SIX MORALE VARIABLES ON ACCULTURATION VARIABLES

Mean percentage indicating:

	Acceptance of Norms				Old-timers as major source of advice and information	Perception of friendliness
	Attitude toward urban settlement	Collective versus individual orientation	Attitude toward free immigration	Attitude toward ethnically mixed housing		
Europeans (time in Israel)						
Low Morale						
Fewer than four months	30	41	70	53	45	58
Four to six months	23	24	68	61	45	35
More than six months	19	26	59	48	34	30
High Morale						
Fewer than four months	37	57	84	68	70	72
Four to six months	27	42	77	65	70	67
More than six months	29	50	75	67	54	51
Non-Europeans (time in Israel)						
Low Morale						
Fewer than four months	14	33	64	64	60	49
Four to six months	19	35	59	72	62	59
More than six months	19	31	73	74	72	58
High Morale						
Fewer than four months	26	46	83	68	72	71
Four to six months	27	48	88	78	77	79
More than six months	29	43	76	83	82	84

persistently show approach, regardless of the level of morale. Among the pessimistic non-Europeans in Table 31, approach appears only on three acculturation variables—"attitude toward ethnically mixed housing," "major source of advice and information," and "attitude toward host society." In the summary table, which reflects the role of all six morale variables, however, the approach pattern appears among the non-Europeans with low morale on all but one acculturation variable, "collective verses individual orientation."

Thus, the over-all approach and withdrawal patterns which characterize the two major ethnic groups operate over and above the effects of morale. The configurations generally appear among those with poor morale as well as among those with good morale. Although it has been shown that high morale fosters an attitude of approach, there are apparently other factors functioning independently to bring about the characteristic acculturation patterns.

SUMMARY

One might have expected an opposite trend in the patterns of acculturation. If one considers the general themes of Israeli culture, especially during the early years of the state, it is evident that it was basically Western. There was little in the culture to indicate that the physical location of the country was at the center of the Middle East. This cultural emphasis shifted somewhat after the great influx of immigrants from Near Eastern and North African countries, but it nevertheless continues to play a dominant role in the over-all value pattern. During the early period, however, the culture of the early European settlers undoubtedly was the basic determinant of the values and social institutions of the young state. Thus, European immigrants might feel more at home in the new society and draw closer to its norms and institutions because of their ostensibly greater familiarity with the culture. The opposite trend observed indicates that cultural similarity of the societies an immigrant is moving into and out of is not an adequate predictor of the structure of acculturation.

In sum, the data indicate that approach is characteristic of the non-European immigrants; withdrawal, of the Europeans. These patterns emerge in observing the acculturation variables over time. Differences in morale between the two ethnic groups partially explain the patterns, but do not provide a complete theory for interpreting them. Thus, as indicated by consistently lower morale, the Europeans feel more "relatively deprived" during their early experiences in Israel. Furthermore, low morale does induce withdrawal among both ethnic groups although a great residue of approach and withdrawal persists in each of the ethnic groups regardless of morale. More specifically, Europeans with high morale tend to show a pattern of withdrawal just as non-Europeans with low morale persist in their pattern of approach. It was, therefore, necessary to conclude that something more than the different levels of morale conditions these two patterns.

It is somewhat easier to propose an explanation for the pattern of the non-Europeans. Here it may be suggested that a desire for social mobility motivates their behavior. Having emigrated from countries in which the social opportunities for Jews were relatively limited, they may sense the relative openness of Israeli society and the possibilities for social mobility which such openness presents. Apparently, the barriers to mobility for non-Europeans are not completely known to them. The pattern of approach may thus be viewed as an attempt to enter Israeli society quickly by conforming—if only externally—to its norms and values in the hope that entry will lead to horizontal and vertical mobility.

Quick conformity to the new norms may also be interpreted as a desire for acceptance and approval on the part of people who have lived for many years under extremely depressed economic and social conditions. The need for such acceptance is likely to be more prevalent among the non-Europeans, who were not always accepted as full citizens in the countries from which they emigrated. Rapid external conformity may thus be interpreted as behavior instrumental to approval and acceptance in Israel. In non-European countries, Western patterns have traditionally been associated with power elites, progress, and economic well-

137

being, so much so that non-Western oriented individuals were likely to develop feelings of cultural inadequacy. In Israel the dominant value system was, at the time, basically Western, and positions of power and authority were occupied largely by people of European origin. It is not surprising, therefore, that the non-Europeans, in consideration of their experience and the social system in which they now found themselves, should make strong efforts to identify with Israeli society, particularly its official norms and values.

The basically religious frame of reference of the non-Europeans may also have played some role in determining their attitudes. The religious orientation of the non-Europeans provided them with a fundamentally positive—in some cases, Messianic—view of the new society. In this respect, they were less likely than the Europeans to perceive flaws and imperfections in Israel, either because of their fundamentally positive attitude or because of their naïveté. This general frame of reference may well have motivated a desire to approach the new social system as rapidly as possible.

I am unable to propose an entirely satisfactory explanation for the withdrawal pattern of the Europeans. The most appropriate single explanation would seem to be the shocked reaction to the bleak conditions of the immigrant transit camps and to the difficulties of getting settled in the new country. The emotional shock of these experiences affected the European immigrant in a manner analogous to physical shock—causing withdrawal from the surrounding environment. The European immigrant, who is shocked by the harshness of the experiences he is undergoing, responds by drawing into himself, rejecting the new society, and diverting his energies from Israeli institutions. Since the physical situation of the immigrants under observation here did not improve very much during their first year in Israel, this reaction functions in a circular, reinforcing manner, causing more withdrawal as time goes on.

Four · Orientation to the Future

9 · Occupational Aspirations

Despite their social suspension in the temporary setting of the transit camp, immigrants were fundamentally concerned with the future: where they would live, what work they would do, what housekeeping would be like in Israel, how comfortably they would be able to live on their salaries, how and where their children would be educated. In the midst of the strain of the transit camp situation, many of these problems may have seemed remote; however, the transit camp was never viewed as a permanent place of settlement, and both the authorities and the immigrants were concerned with the future.

Of all the problems which concerned the immigrant during this period of transition, future occupation seems to be the central one. This chapter will focus on the factors leading immigrants to choose an occupation.

OCCUPATIONAL ASPIRATIONS

In a time of widespread unemployment when most immigrants have not entered the occupational system of the host society, one way to study the problem of occupational choice is to determine occupational aspirations. In effect, this is the only procedure possible as long as the immigrant does not have a regular job in the new society. Even for those fortunate enough to find employment during this period, the problem is not settled, for the first job is frequently not the sort in which the worker expects to remain. It is more often a stopgap than a choice reflecting the immigrant's occupational intentions. And, of course, the low status of the unemployed tells nothing of his future occupational plans. One solution to these difficulties, therefore, is to study job aspirations.

The occupational aspirations of immigrants, however, might well be colored by the strain of unemployment. The depressing effect of unemployment might limit the breadth of occupational aspirations so that immigrants would find it difficult to express their aspirations for a job freely. Such depression might result in a partial repression of occupational aspirations. In addition, unemployment might also bind respondents closer to reality than they would be under favorable circumstances. Immigrants might find it difficult to visualize a situation in which they could get jobs freely, according to their qualifications. During a period when the best they were offered were unskilled jobs, frequently requiring manual labor, prolonged unemployment might so condition immigrants that they found it difficult to imagine a favorable Israeli labor market.

One way of freeing the respondent from the limitations of depression and the bonds of reality is to increase the projective nature of the question by trying to determine the immigrant's aspirations for his son's future occupation rather than his own. This procedure permits complete freedom of expression, since it does not focus on the immediate future and is not directly bound to the immigrant's present unemployment. It also has the other advantages of a projective technique in that it provides an insight into the immigrant's image of Israeli society and his entry into its occupational structure.

At the same time, using respondents' aspirations for their sons' future occupation involves a number of difficulties in that certain extraneous factors not necessarily related to the problem at hand are thereby introduced into the analysis. In particular, there is the problem of the parent-son relationship, which may include any number of complications concerning the stability of that relationship and the possible projection of personality needs of the parent onto his son. In addition, although it frees the respondent from the reality of the unemployment situation, it may boomerang by making him entirely unrealistic. This reaction would be most likely among respondents with very young children, for whom occupation is a problem in the distant future.

Nevertheless, in weighing the pros and cons of the case, I decided to use aspirations for sons' occupations because I believed that it was most important to free the immigrant from the limitations imposed by unemployment and to encourage the broadest expression of occupational aspirations. This should produce a variety of data consisting of a wide assortment of aspirations for future occupations. In considering these data, however, it is important to bear in mind the limitations stemming from the nature of the material itself.

Thus it may be seen that certain limitations of the situation caused me to focus the data in a way that defined the original problem somewhat differently. Rather than being concerned with the immediate occupational aspirations of the immigrants, I ask about their image of future, more permanent entry into the occupational structure of the new society, thereby gaining an indirect insight into the immigrant's picture of the Israeli occupational structure and the place he hopes his son will take in it.

The basic question on which the material in this chapter is based was formulated as follows: What occupation would you like your eldest son to engage in when he grows up? I decided to ask about sons rather than children in order to avoid the complications of attitudes toward working women, marriage of daughters, and so on. In cases where the question was not entirely meaningful to a respondent because he had no children or no sons or because his son was dead or already had an occupation, interviewers were instructed to formulate the question in more projective terms: "If you had a son, . . ." or "If your son were not already grown and working, . . ." Despite the problematical wording of such questions, it is of interest to note that only 7 per cent of the respondents had no opinion or were unable to answer the questions.

Table 33 lists the occupations the immigrants chose for their

TABLE 33

IMMIGRANTS' CHOICES OF OCCUPATIONS

FOR THEIR ELDEST SONS

Occupation	Number of choices
Skilled craftsman (carpenter, tailor, and so on)	404
Agricultural worker	244
Mechanic	235
White-collar office worker	201
Doctor	188
Engineer	168
Professional (other than doctor or engineer)	77
Businessman	66
Soldier, policeman	56
Member of a collective settlement (*kibbutz*)	19
Other occupations	49
No opinion or no answer	159
Total	1,866

sons. For obvious reasons, there were no unskilled jobs listed. In Table 34 I have collapsed the occupations into four general groups. There is a certain *ad hoc*—although very rough—ranking implied in the order of the occupations in Table 34. The fluid condition of Israeli society at this time made it difficult, if not impossible, to rank occupations clearly. In effect, only the first three groups of occupations can really be thought of in terms of status ranking. Agriculture and *kibbutz,* although of high status for certain segments of the population, would not be universally considered the highest-status position in the society.

The immigrants' lack of familiarity with the country blurs the status implications of their occupational choices; they may not yet be fully aware of the status of a given job in the occupational hierarchy of Israel. Furthermore, they may be imputing a mistaken status to their chosen occupation owing to a carry-over from the occupational system of their country of origin.

TABLE 34

RANK OF OCCUPATIONS CHOSEN FOR SONS

	Percentage	Number
Crafts and trade	38	705
White-collar work, Army	14	257
Professions	23	433
Agriculture and *kibbutz*	14	263
Other or no answer	11	208
	100	1,866

The most frequent choice is crafts and trades with 38 per cent of the immigrants choosing that category. Next come the professions, with 23 per cent. It is of some interest to note that the latter are second in frequency despite the projective framework of the questions and despite the traditional emphasis on this type of occupation in many of the immigrants' countries of origin. White collar and Army and agriculture and *kibbutz* appear in third place, with frequencies of 14 per cent. It is striking that agriculture and *kibbutz* are as frequently chosen as white-collar occupations, a phenomenon which seems to indicate sensitivity to the Israeli goals of pioneering and collective orientation.

Agriculture and *kibbutz* represent ideologically oriented occupations in Israel. The Zionist ethic, with its emphasis on pioneering and its rejection of traditional Jewish occupations, has placed a moral premium on occupations which further these goals. Farming in particular has been accorded a high moral status in the Israeli occupational structure on the assumption that it, more than any other single occupation, conforms to the Zionist ethic. At the same time, the ideological values associated with agriculture and the *kibbutz* are not universally esteemed by all segments of the population.

What Determines Occupational Choice?

Do men and women immigrants differ in their occupational aspirations? It will be recalled that both men and women were asked to state their aspirations for their sons' occupations. For men this question involves a fairly simple role identification; women, however, must project beyond a sex-role boundary. Apparently, this boundary did not inhibit responses, since there were no differences between men and women in the proportion of those unable to answer the question (8 per cent in both cases).

It is of interest to ask whether this projection resulted in any other differences in the responses of the women. Table 35 indi-

---

TABLE 35

OCCUPATIONS CHOSEN BY MEN AND WOMEN IMMIGRANTS

	Crafts and trades	White-collar and Army jobs	Pro-fessions	Agri-culture and *kibbutz* work	Other *		
Percentage							
Men	42	12	21	15	10	(1,007)	$\chi^2 = 25.03$
							D.F. $= 4$
Women	33	16	25	13	13	(859)	P $< .001$

* "Other" includes "no answer."

---

cates that there are a number of differences between men and women in their choices of occupations. Men tend more to choose the crafts and trades, whereas women choose the professions and white-collar and Army jobs. There is no difference between the sexes in choices of agriculture and *kibbutz*.

How does the introduction of additional background variables affect the general configuration observed in Table 35? [1] I shall first observe the choice of crafts and trades in somewhat greater detail.

Table 36 indicates that age and education, as well as sex, condition the choice of crafts and trades. Less-educated and older respondents tend more to choose these occupations. The fact that less-educated respondents tend to select relatively low-status occupations shows the repressive function of a low-status position on future aspirations, for it may be assumed that the less-educated immigrants are probably in low-status positions. The role of education and age both point to the limitations which the immigrant's present status sets, even for his aspirations about his son's occupation. Ethnic origin plays no role in determining the choice of crafts and trades.

TABLE 36

CHOICE OF CRAFTS AND TRADES
BY SEX, AGE, AND EDUCATION

| | Less education | | More education | |
	Younger	Older	Younger	Older
	Percentage			
Men	37 (342)	54 (307)	35 (194)	38 (160)
Women	32 (361)	47 (206)	20 (209)	34 (76)

Further analysis of those aspiring to white-collar and Army jobs shows that ethnic background, as well as sex conditions these aspirations. No other background variable observed has a significant effect. In Table 37 it can be seen that educational background plays no role in the configuration, whereas ethnic background and sex do: non-Europeans in all subgroups are more likely to select white-collar or Army jobs than are Europeans, and women are slightly, but consistently, prone to make such a choice. One explanation for this phenomenon may be the relative oc-

[1] In this table and in Tables 37 and 38, I have not carried out standard significance tests. The relations described in the text may be seen on the tables in the remarkable consistency revealed by the data when the relevant percentages are compared systematically, generally two at a time.

cupational immobility of Jews in the Moslem countries. The Arab countries, as compared to the European countries, were more occupationally immobile, and this immobility was felt particularly by the Jews. This situation often resulted in occupations of such medium status as white-collar jobs, teaching, government posts representing the highest-status occupations available to Jews. In time such jobs came to represent the highest-status occupations open to them, and their aspirations were directed accordingly. White-collar jobs may, therefore, represent occupations with high status for the non-European immigrants.

TABLE 37

CHOICE OF WHITE-COLLAR AND ARMY JOBS BY SEX, ETHNIC BACKGROUND, AND EDUCATION

| | Europeans | | Non-Europeans | |
	Less education	More education	Less education	More education
	Percentage			
Men	6 (191)	6 (218)	16 (458)	15 (136)
Women	11 (156)	9 (207)	21 (411)	22 (80)

Four background variables—sex, age, education, and ethnic origin—play a role in determining the choice of the professions. Younger, better-educated immigrants are more likely to choose the professions for their sons. These are the people least likely to be limited in their occupational aspirations. However, when age, education, and ethnic background are held constant, it appears —although not entirely consistently—that sex conditions the choice among Europeans but not among non-Europeans. Among the Europeans, women (in three of the four subgroups in Table 38) chose the professions more frequently than men; however, among the non-Europeans, there is no such tendency (in three of the four subgroups of Table 38). There is also a tendency among the Europeans, particularly the women, to favor the professions more than non-Europeans do, although here again the trend is not entirely consistent (six of the eight subgroups). The number of cases in some of the subgroups of Table 38 is so small that our conclusions concerning this configuration can be only tentative.

TABLE 38

CHOICE OF THE PROFESSIONS BY SEX, ETHNIC
BACKGROUND, EDUCATION, AND AGE

	Europeans			
	Less education		More education	
	Younger	Older	Younger	Older
	Percentage			
Men	22 (65)	14 (126)	27 (103)	33 (115)
Women	32 (66)	24 (90)	46 (151)	24 (55)

	Non-Europeans			
	Less education		More education	
	Younger	Older	Younger	Older
	Percentage			
Men	23 (277)	9 (181)	31 (91)	18 (45)
Women	19 (295)	5 (116)	41 (58)	19 (21)

The two principal findings—that non-Europeans are more likely to choose white-collar occupations and Europeans are more likely to choose the professions—may be better understood in view of certain aspects of the Israeli occupational structure and the opportunities it makes available to members of the two ethnic groups. Although all occupations are theoretically open to all, there is reason to believe that differences in educational background as well as other economic and social barriers make it more difficult for non-Europeans to enter high-status occupations. This reality operates despite the fairly strong formal equalitarianism. It is conceivable that non-European immigrants, although they have not been in Israel long, are sensitive to these differing opportunities and revise their occupational goals accordingly, selecting white-collar jobs rather than the professions.

There is no evidence that the choice of agriculture or the

TABLE 39

EFFECT OF ZIONISM ON OCCUPATIONAL ASPIRATIONS
BY ETHNIC BACKGROUND AND SEX

	Crafts and trades	White-collar and Army jobs	Professions	Agriculture and kibbutz	Other	
			Percentage			
Europeans						
Men						
Zionists	45	6	24	15	10	(265)
Non-Zionists	41	7	24	11	17	(143)
Women						
Zionists	28	12	34	17	9	(191)
Non-Zionists	35	8	36	6	15	(168)
						$\chi^2 = 14.73$ D.F. $= 4$ .01 $>$ P $>$ .001
Non-Europeans						
Men						
Zionists	32	17	20	23	8	(163)
Non-Zionists	44	15	17	13	11	(432)
Women						
Zionists	27	18	30	18	7	(33)
Non-Zionists	35	21	18	14	12	(453)
						$\chi^2 = 13.60$ D.F. $= 4$ .01 $>$ P $>$ .001

TABLE 40

EFFECT OF IMMIGRANTS' ORIENTATION TOWARD THE FUTURE ON OCCUPATIONAL ASPIRATIONS

BY ETHNIC BACKGROUND AND SEX

	Crafts and trades	White-collar and Army jobs	Professions	Agriculture and *kibbutz*	Other		
			Percentage				
Europeans							
Men							
Optimists	42	8	24	16	10	(244)	$\chi^2 = 11.12$
							D.F. $= 4$
Pessimists	48	4	24	8	16	(164)	$.05 > P > .02$
Women							
Optimists	31	7	36	16	10	(208)	$\chi^2 = 13.44$
							D.F. $= 4$
Pessimists	32	15	33	6	14	(149)	$.02 > P > .01$
Non-Europeans							
Men							
Optimists	40	16	20	17	7	(508)	
Pessimists	41	16	20	10	13	(86)	
Women							
Optimists	35	22	15	16	12	(394)	$\chi^2 = 15.95$
							D.F. $= 4$
Pessimists	35	17	31	9	8	(93)	$.01 > P > .001$

kibbutz is conditioned by any of the personal background variables observed.

The Role of Ideology

How does a background of Zionist commitment condition the immigrant's occupational aspirations for his son?

The only really clear impression to emerge from Table 39 concerns the role of Zionism on the choice of agriculture and *kibbutz:* more immigrants with an ideological background of Zionism select these idealistic occupational goals.[2] Other than this conclusion, the evidence on the role of Zionism is rather unclear. One gets the impression that an ideological background tends to reduce the choice of crafts and trades, but here again the data are not entirely consistent or statistically significant.

The Immigrant's Outlook

A scale on immigrants' general optimism or pessimism about their futures in Israel was included in the study. This is the same scale used in Chapter 6 to analyze the effects of the Nazi concentration camp on response to new strain. How does the general orientation toward the future affect occupational aspirations? In effect, I am dealing with the relation between a general and a specific form of orientation toward the future.

Here again, with the exception of the choice of agriculture and *kibbutz,* the evidence in Table 40 is unclear. The percentage differences are small and inconsistent. The only clear-cut evidence to emerge from this table concerns the effect of an optimistic orientation on idealistic occupational choices: optimists in all subgroups show a higher choice of agriculture and *kibbutz* than do pessimists.

Both Zionist ideology and optimism have been shown to increase the immigrant's choice of an idealistic occupation. The question remains whether these two variables operate independently or whether they are associated in a way that makes the

[2] In order to simplify the table and reduce the number of subgroups, the scale on Zionism was divided here into only two groups—"Zionists" and "non-Zionists."

previous observations spurious. Table 41 indicates that both Zionist ideology and optimism do function independently to increase the choice of agriculture and *kibbutz*.

TABLE 41

EFFECT OF ZIONISM AND ORIENTATION TOWARD FUTURE
ON CHOICE OF AGRICULTURE AND "KIBBUTZ"

	Percentage	
Zionists		
Optimists	21	(454)
Pessimists	10	(199)
Non-Zionists		
Optimists	14	(896)
Pessimists	7	(300)

Among "optimists"
χ^2 for effect of "Zionism" $= 10.78$
$$D.F. = 1$$
$$.01 > P > .001$$

Among "pessimists"
χ^2 for effect of "Zionism" $= 1.44$
$$D.F. = 1$$
$$.30 > P > .20$$

Among "Zionists"
χ^2 for effect of "optimism" $= 11.21$
$$D.F. = 1$$
$$P < .001$$

Among "Non-Zionists"
χ^2 for effect of "optimism" $= 10.10$
$$D.F. = 1$$
$$P < .001$$

SUMMARY

This chapter has attempted to project the immigrant into the future. It has been based on data concerning immigrants' aspirations for their sons' future occupations. The specific occupations were roughly ranged in an ascending hierarchy of four groups, as follows: crafts and trades, white-collar and Army jobs, professions, and agriculture and *kibbutz*. Agriculture and *kibbutz* represent idealistic occupations in the Israeli cultural context.

When the effect of the immigrants' personal background characteristics on occupational aspirations was examined, it was found that two basic sociological variables could best explain the configurations observed: sex and certain elements in the social structures of the countries of origin. The evidence points to an emphasis on crafts and trades among men and an emphasis on white-collar jobs and the professions among women. Europeans tend to be more status-oriented, selecting the professions, whereas non-Europeans are more oriented to white-collar jobs and the Army. This phenomenon was explained by reference to the differing opportunities open to Jews in the European and non-European countries: in the latter, it was suggested that the relative immobility of the occupational system resulted in non-European immigrants' aspiring to white-collar occupations which are low-ranking, since these occupations were the highest-ranking ones formerly open to them. The precariousness of life in the non-European countries might have resulted in a need for the kind of security offered by a white-collar job. Finally, the non-Europeans, despite the relatively brief period they have been in Israel, may have sensed the barriers which work against them in Israel and thus adjusted their aspirations accordingly.

The effect of the immigrant's commitment to Zionism was also examined for its role in conditioning occupational aspirations. The evidence points to a stronger idealistic orientation among immigrants with a background of ideological commitment, but, other than this, such a commitment appears to play no role. The same general conclusion applies to the immigrant's general outlook. The data indicate that optimism induces a stronger idealistic orientation, but, other than this, optimism seems to exert no discernible effect on occupational aspirations.

10 · Aspirations for Mobility

This chapter continues to project the immigrant into the future. How do aspirations for sons' occupations compare with their fathers' occupations before coming to Israel? Rather than deal with specific job changes, I shall compare the status of the two occupations to see whether a father aspires to more for his son, whether he will be satisfied to have his son occupy about the same status in Israel that he himself had occupied in his country of origin, or whether he is idealistic in the sense that he is willing to consider an occupation of lower social status than the one he had.

OCCUPATIONAL CHANGE AND SOCIAL STRUCTURE

Immigration almost always involves considerable occupational change for the newcomers. This change stems partially

from differences between the occupational structure of
tries of origin and the receiving society. Also, Jews in thei
countries of origin were characterized by a unique occu{
situation which generally did not conform to the broa\
cupational system of those countries or of Israel.[1] These
ences inevitably call for occupational mobility on the pa ̄
immigrants. Such mobility is, in a sense, a product of imm
tion, which, in the case of Israel, introduced much economic
location into the social system. Certain types of occupations w\
suddenly oversupplied, whereas others were scarce. Despite e
perience in similar jobs, immigrants were often unable to perforn
occupational roles in the manner expected in the new society;
professional requirements of certain occupations were different,
so that some immigrants could not pursue their usual jobs despite
formal qualifications.

Israeli culture is ideally characterized by an ideological orientation to the occupational system which grew from a desire to
"normalize" Jewish economic life by redistributing occupations;
thus, a high value was placed on manual occupations of all sorts,
particularly agricultural ones, and the more traditional occupations of Jews—trade, shopkeeping, the professions—were somewhat deprecated. This value system brought pressure to bear on
immigrants, urging them to settle in rural communities and become farmers rather than pursue the occupations they had prac-
ticed in their countries of origin.

In this regard, it is interesting to note that only 34 per cent
of the immigrants indicated any interest in agriculture, whereas
60 per cent favored shopkeeping as their occupational choice (see
Appendix A). In addition, only 17 per cent report having heard
anything from the information campaign run by the settlement
authorities about the opportunities offered to those willing to
become farmers (see Appendix A). Thus, it is clear that an im-
balance existed between the occupational intentions of the immigrants and the values of the Israeli leadership.

[1] See Arieh Tartokower, *Hachevra Hayehudit* (Tel Aviv and Jerusalem:
Massada, 1957), especially chap. 5; also Sicron, *op. cit.*, chap. x.

Israeli society has crystallized, during the brief period of its existence, into a markedly open social system.[2] There are few structural barriers to upward mobility—there is no entrenched upper class, class differences are insignificant owing to the relatively slight salary differences and the progressive tax system, equalitarianism is strong and widespread, there is free and universal elementary schooling, and inexpensive trade schools are widely available. These equalizing factors have weakened considerably since the establishment of the state, but during the early years they played a more dominant role. It is unlikely that a fully institutionalized, Western-oriented society will be able to maintain such structural equalitarianism on a stable basis for a long time. Furthermore, there were few inbred prejudices against specific groups in the population, although a certain amount of negative feeling has developed against some of the non-European ethnic groups.[3] The latter does hinder mobility for the members of such groups. However, the major structural factor that prevents the complete openness of the society is the fact that secondary and higher education not only are not free, but also are extremely expensive. Also, there are not sufficient scholarships to permit all qualified students to continue their education.

Despite the fact that Israel may be characterized as a generally open society, upward mobility has not been a dominant value in the culture, as it has in the United States, for example. Although in recent years it is coming to occupy an increasingly important place in the value system, it is still not a principal motivating factor in conditioning most behavior. In the occupational sphere, pioneering, more particularly agriculture, has been the occupation on which the highest value has traditionally been placed by the culture; this emphasis, however, has shifted in recent years particularly since the establishment of the state. It is my impression that, during the early years of the state, the empha-

[2] Eisenstadt, *op. cit.*, chap. III.
[3] Judith T. Shuval, "Patterns of Intergroup Tension and Affinity," *International Social Science Bulletin, UNESCO*, VIII, No. 1 (1956), 75–123; *idem*, "Ethnic Stereotyping in Israeli Medical Bureaucracies," *Sociology and Social Research*, XLVI, No. 4 (1962); *idem*, "Emerging Patterns of Ethnic Strain in Israel," *Social Forces*, XL, No. 4 (1962), 323–330.

sis shifted toward security as a major occupational goal, perhaps as a result of the influx of many non-European immigrants or for deeper psychological reasons which cannot be analyzed now. This value manifested itself during this period in a desire among young and old for permanent employment, particularly for jobs giving pension rights and other social benefits. In any case, in considering this problem, it should be recalled that the population with which I am dealing consists of immigrants who have been in Israel for a brief time and have had little opportunity to become sensitive to the values of the prevailing culture. As time has passed, however, occupational interests have shifted to the professions and other high-income jobs. This shift has been accompanied by a gradual weakening of equalitarianism.

Equally important is the relative openness of the societies from which the immigrants came. To the extent that values concerning social mobility have been internalized by the immigrant, they have been acquired from the culture of his country of origin and conditioned by the extent to which mobility was possible there. For example, an immigrant from a Middle Eastern country which had little social mobility finds himself in a new social situation where upward mobility is within his realm of possibility. His reaction is likely to be quite different from that of an immigrant who was socialized in an open, mobile society. Generally, whatever the mobility in the various countries of origin, the system was almost invariably more closed to Jews than to non-Jews. In the Moslem countries limitations in occupational opportunities for Jews were rigidly institutionalized and legitimized by religious prescription. In the Middle Eastern countries subject to some Western influence, such as Egypt and Iraq, these limitations were less extreme; in the countries under a traditional Moslem system, such as Yemen, however, they were strictly enforced.

The situation differed in the various European countries according to the extent that anti-Semitism limited occupational mobility for Jews. With the exception of Nazi Germany, no countries institutionalized their anti-Semitic practices in the occupational sphere as the Moslem countries did. Nevertheless, severe limitations on upward mobility were common and were expressed by a *numerus clausus* at the universities, discrimination in hiring and firing, social barriers, and, not infrequently, open hostility.

It is against this background—the relatively open Israeli society and the various limitations of the countries from which the newcomers had emigrated—that the question of mobility must be considered.

Mobility

Mobility was defined by a comparison of the former occupations of immigrant fathers with the occupations to which they aspire for their sons. The present chapter is based on data obtained from male respondents only ($N = 1,007$). Table 42 presents the distribution of the fathers' occupations in their countries of origin, and Table 43 presents the distribution of occupations to which they aspire for their sons.

TABLE 42

FATHERS' OCCUPATIONS BEFORE IMMIGRATING TO ISRAEL

Occupation	Number of choices
Skilled craft (carpentry, weaving, shoemaking, and so on)	401
Business or trade	265
White-collar work	132
Unskilled labor	57
Study	23
Shopkeeping	21
Agriculture	16
Profession	12
Owner of Factory	11
Rabbinate and other religious functions	7
Teaching	6
No regular occupation	16
Other occupations	39
No answer	1
Total	1,007

Cross tabulation of the distributions in Table 42 and Table 43 classified the men into four categories: (1) "upward mobile,"

(2) "similar status," (3) "downward mobile (idealism)," and (4) "unclassifiable." A father whose aspiration for his son was an occupation that has higher status than his own, requires greater skill and training, and demands more education, has been defined "upward mobile." A father whose aspiration is an occupation of a status similar to his own in his country of origin has been classified "similar status." Immigrants who aspire to occupations of lower status than their own have been classified "downward mobile." The last category has meaning only in the Israeli context, where agricultural and manual occupations have acquired a unique status because of the value pioneering has in this culture.

TABLE 43

CHOICES OF OCCUPATIONS BY IMMIGRANT
FATHERS FOR THEIR ELDEST SONS

Occupation	Number of choices
Skilled craft	236
Metal trades	156
Agriculture	137
Medicine	95
Engineering	87
White-collar work	86
Professions (other than medicine or engineering)	35
Army or police force	32
Business or trade	30
Kibbutz	11
Other occupations	30
No opinion or no answer	72
Total	1,007

One of the major problems of such a classification stems from the different occupational status hierarchies in the immigrants' countries of origin. An occupation may rank high in one culture and low in another, making the comparison of aspirations with former occupations somewhat difficult. Another problem is the immigrant's perception of the Israeli occupational status system and how he classifies the occupation to which he aspires in its hierarchy. Since the immigrants have been in the country for so brief a period and are living under such isolated conditions, their opportunities for getting acquainted with the Israeli status system are markedly limited. Furthermore, the status hierarchy of Israeli society was comparatively uncrystallized at this time because the social system was undergoing fundamental changes as a result of mass immigration.

These problems resulted in ambiguity in the classification of some aspirations. The procedure in uncertain cases was to stay on the side of caution, placing the aspiration in the unclassifiable category. Sixteen per cent of the cases were unclassifiable (Table 44); this large percentage reflects the conservatism exercised in classification. The aspirations that were placed in the other three groups were fairly clear-cut cases. Thus, for example, upward mobile people included skilled craftsmen who aspired to the professions, unskilled laborers who aspired to white-collar jobs or the skilled crafts, white-collar workers who aspired to the professions, and so on. Similar status consisted of men who chose the same profession or category of profession for their sons and those who chose occupations which seemed to be of the same status as their own jobs. Downward mobility is meaningful only because of the Israeli pioneering ethic; it included all choices of agriculture and *kibbutz* except those of the few immigrants who had been agricultural workers or unskilled laborers or had not had a regular occupation. Former teachers and white-collar workers who wanted their sons to be mechanics and white-collar workers who wanted their sons to be skilled craftsmen were also classified downward mobile (idealism). I have not entered into the question of distance between the father's and the son's occupation largely to avoid the very complicated problem of defining the intervals. Thus any choice of a higher-ranking occupation for the son was considered upward mobile, regardless of its distance from the father's job.

In its concern with any mobility rather than upward mobility, this approach differs somewhat from that followed in most studies of occupational mobility. In such studies an attempt is usually made to locate factors which cause a choice of high-ranking occupations or a behavior that would be likely to lead to such occupations. Thus the criteria used have often included such variables as scholastic achievement, intention to go to college, and so on.[4] I, on the other hand, am concerned with any movement, even if it is that of an unskilled laborer aspiring to a skilled job for his son. In the sense used here, a doctor who hopes his son will also enter the medical profession is not upward mobile. I am concerned with the factors that condition a man to aspire to a job different from his own for his son.[5]

TABLE 44

DIRECTION OF MOBILITY OF FATHERS' OCCUPATIONAL
ASPIRATIONS FOR THEIR SONS

	Upward mobile	Similar status	Downward mobile (idealism)	Unclassifiable	Total
Number	278	384	178	162	1,002
Percentage	28	38	18	16	100

The difference in approach becomes more graphic if we consider the role of class position in mobility as defined here. Class has generally been found to act as a useful predictor of mobility: the higher a man's class, the higher his aspiration. In the present case, however, class operates in the opposite direction. Since upper-class people are generally more satisfied with their occupations, they display less upward mobility than do lower-class people, who may not aspire to very high-status jobs but who do want their sons to move upward. Furthermore, there is a ceiling: the higher a man's class, the fewer his opportunities for

[4] See, for example, Elbridge Sibley, "Some Demographic Clues to Stratification," *American Sociological Review*, VII, (June 1942), 322–330.
[5] I have not here entered into the problem of what means, if any, will be mobilized in order to realize this aspiration for the son. I am concerned more with the attitudinal aspect of the aspiration than with its realization. However, the introduction of an additional variable, "intention to carry out the aspiration" would serve as a useful problem for additional research.

upward mobility. Thus, the upper-class immigrants do show less upward mobility than members of the lower-class groups.

Background Factors and Mobility

What factors in the immigrants' backgrounds play a role in conditioning his occupational aspirations? In Table 45 the data are arranged according to the effects of four basic background variables: ethnic origin, age, education, and length of time in Israel.

TABLE 45

EFFECTS OF ETHNIC ORIGIN, AGE, EDUCATION,

AND LENGTH OF TIME IN ISRAEL

ON OCCUPATIONAL ASPIRATIONS

	Upward mobile	Similar status	Down-ward mobile	Unclas-sifiable	
	Percentage				
Ethnic origin					
Europeans	23	39	18	20	(408)
Non-Europeans	31	38	17	14	(591)
Age					
Under forty	31	35	18	16	(535)
Over forty	24	42	18	16	(464)
Education					
Fewer than six years of school	27	44	12	17	(644)
More than six years of school	29	29	22	20	(352)
Time in Israel					
Fewer than four months	29	35	18	18	(274)
More than four months	28	40	18	14	(725)

Of the four background variables examined only one—length of time in Israel—plays no role in conditioning the direction of occupational mobility. The remaining three all have some effect, although it is not always very strong. The non-

Europeans are more upward mobile than the Europeans. This ethnic difference is rather important in understanding the general picture of occupational mobility. Younger immigrants are more upward mobile and less likely to aspire to their own status than older immigrants. And, finally, the better-educated men in the population are more often classified downward mobile (idealism) and are less likely to seek their own status than the less-educated respondents. The role of the background variables persists when their joint effect on aspirations is observed.

It is, of course, possible that the greater upward mobility on the part of the non-Europeans can be attributed to their clustering in the low-income groups. I have already pointed out that the lower-class groups are distinguished by stronger aspirations for upward mobility. The data show that lower- and middle-class non-Europeans indicate more frequent upward mobility than do Europeans. This trend, however, does not appear in the highest class, so that with the exception of the high-class non-Europeans, the finding of Table 45 holds: non-Europeans are somewhat more upward mobile than Europeans, although the differences are not great. The absence of upward mobility in the highest class is probably accounted for by the fact that those who have reached the highest class have fewer opportunities for upward mobility since there are fewer occupations above them. Also, the non-Europeans who have attained a higher-class position have less need to compensate for the difficulties of occupational mobility in their countries of origin.

How does the immigrant's present employment status affect his occupational aspirations? The major reason for using aspirations for son's occupation rather than for the respondent's future job was to avoid the possibly depressing and repressive effects of unemployment on aspirations. Is there any evidence that unemployment exerts a depressing effect on the respondent's aspirations for his son? According to Table 46, the respondent's present employment status exerts no discernible effect on his aspirations for his son's future occupation. In a sense, then, I have overcome the possibly depressing effects of current unemployment on the expression of aspirations by focusing on the son rather than on the respondent, although I have no empirical evidence that such an effect would have occurred. I can note only that it does not occur here.

TABLE 46

EFFECT OF EMPLOYMENT STATUS

ON OCCUPATIONAL MOBILITY

	Upward mobile	Similar status	Down-ward mobile	Unclas-sifiable	
	P e r c e n t a g e				
Employed	27	40	19	14	(304)
Unemployed	28	38	17	17	(692)

Immigrants view their present employment status as something temporary which is inherent in their adjustment to a new country, as, indeed, it was in most cases. This impression stems from the fact that morale as defined by personal adjustment is not significantly affected by the immigrant's employment status: among the employed, 16 per cent (306) is characterized by poor personal adjustment; among the unemployed, 21 per cent (695) is characterized by poor personal adjustment. This difference is not statistically significant.[6] The relationship between morale and unemployment, however, is essentially not a direct one, but one mediated by an assortment of reference groups from which the immigrant acquires norms of employment expectations.

ACTIVITY-PASSIVITY

A factor that plays a role in determining occupational aspirations was defined by a variable called "activity-passivity." This variable refers to the extent that the individual generally accepts his over-all situation and is willing to be moved by forces over which he is likely to have little control. "Active" people are those who feel a need to take a more positive role in controlling their

---

[6] $Sigma_d = .027$, $P = .14$.

place in the social system: rather than accepting their momentary location as given, they seek actively to adapt it to their own needs. A series of questions asked the immigrant how anxious he was to get out of the temporary transit camp. (In Appendix A this scale is called "general acceptance of the camp situation.") Viewing the emerging scale in its more general sense, I assumed that those who expressed a great need to leave the temporary transit camp are more "active" and that those who are willing to bide their time without making any special effort to move out are relatively "passive." The total population split into 60 per cent who generally accepted the camp situation and 40 per cent who did not (see Appendix A). However, for the purposes of the present chapter, I observed only the men in the population and found that only 53 per cent accepted the camp situation and 47 per cent did not.

Table 47 shows the role played by activity-passivity in occupational aspirations. Active people tend to be more upward mobile, aspiring less to occupations of their own status level than do passive people. There is no difference between the active and passive in downward mobility (idealism).

TABLE 47

EFFECT OF ACTIVITY-PASSIVITY ON

OCCUPATIONAL ASPIRATIONS

	Upward mobile	Similar status	Downward mobile	Unclassifiable		
	Percentage					
Active	32	35	18	15	(469)	$\chi^2 = 8.74$
						D.F. $= 3$
Passive	24	41	18	17	(530)	$.05 > P > .02$

The effect of activity-passivity is small but consistent: it appears among practically all subgroups of the population examined. Table 48, for example, shows its operation among class and ethnic subgroups. With the exception of the lowest-class

Europeans, who are too few to yield a reliable statistic, the active are always more upward mobile than the passive. Although the differences between the active and the passive are not all statistically significant, it is the consistency of the relationship that interests us. Among the four sets of subgroups where comparison is possible, three show the passive to aspire more to their own status position than the active. In addition to showing the role of activity-passivity in conditioning aspirations, Table 48 also confirms the previously noted finding that non-Europeans tend to be

TABLE 48

EFFECT OF ACTIVITY-PASSIVITY ON OCCUPATIONAL ASPIRATIONS AMONG CLASS AND ETHNIC GROUPS

	Upward mobile	Similar status	Downward mobile	Unclassifiable	
	P e r c e n t a g e				
Europeans					
Lowest class					
Active	60	—	—	40	(5)
Passive	100	—	—	—	(6)
Middle class					
Active	35	51	9	5	(75)
Passive	21	46	14	19	(57)
Highest class					
Active	22	39	29	10	(129)
Passive	19	46	22	13	(97)
Non-Europeans					
Lowest class					
Active	92	—	—	8	(25)
Passive	81	—	—	19	(21)
Middle class					
Active	43	39	13	5	(95)
Passive	29	47	18	6	(174)
Highest class					
Active	26	39	26	9	(105)
Passive	18	47	23	12	(137)

more upward mobile than Europeans. This tendency can be seen in all subgroups of reliable size with the exception, as already noted, of the highest-class passive group.

The role of "activity-passivity" in determining occupational aspirations assumes a heightened significance in view of other theoretical work in this general area. Joseph A. Kahl has pointed to the crucial significance of parental pressure on the upward mobility of high school boys and has observed that among "common man" families this pressure is, to a large measure, a function of two different value systems which appear to characterize these families. These value systems he calls "getting by" and "getting ahead." [7] Families characterized by "getting by" accept their own style of life without much concern for basic changes in it; they are satisfied to view the future as a continuation of the present and do not feel a marked need for improvement. Although they may not view their own standard of living as the best that might be attained, they are, nevertheless, satisfied to have it continue on much the same level since they do not consider themselves qualified for higher positions. Generally speaking, such families are not upward mobile, nor do they tend to pressure their sons to aspire higher. Families characterized by "getting ahead" generally feel that they could or should be living better than they are and that, with a certain amount of effort, they can rise to the desired level. Often the father feels that for one reason or another he was denied the opportunity to get as far ahead as he might have, and this frustration is manifested by pressure on his son to acquire the training needed to get ahead. Such families are upward mobile.[8]

The "activity-passivity" variable bears a strong resemblance to Kahl's "getting ahead" and "getting by." The active-passive reference, however, is relevant not only to the particular style of life which the family has attained, but also to its general position in the social system. The findings of this chapter concerning the greater upward mobility of the active tend to confirm the significance of the parallel between the two concepts, although additional research is needed to clarify the relation.

[7] Joseph A. Kahl, "Educational and Occupational Aspirations of 'Common Man' Boys," *The Harvard Educational Review*, XXIII, No. 3 (1953), 186–203.
[8] *Ibid.*, pp. 192–196.

Having demonstrated the importance of activity-passivity in determining occupational aspirations, I deemed it useful to explore this variable more fully. To do this, I attempted to discover which factors determine whether a person is active or passive.

The first important background factor which determines an immigrant's tendency toward activity or passivity is his ethnic background. Europeans are significantly more active than non-Europeans. This basic difference between Europeans and non-Europeans holds among age and educational level groups as well as among people who have been in Israel for differing lengths of time. Table 49, for example, indicates the activity-passivity of

TABLE 49

ACTIVITY AS RELATED TO ETHNIC BACKGROUND, EDUCATION, AND LENGTH OF TIME IN ISRAEL

	Europeans		Non-Europeans	
	Percentage			
More than seven grades				
More than six months in Israel	68	(148)	55	(55)
Fewer than six months in Israel	59	(70)	47	(81)
Fewer than seven grades				
More than six months in Israel	51	(125)	40	(193)
Fewer than six months in Israel	45	(66)	33	(264)

Europeans and non-Europeans among groups of similar education and length of time in Israel. All subgroup comparisons show greater activity among the Europeans. Shumsky notes a similar difference between the Oriental and Ashkenazi communities.[9] A level of activity or passivity appears to characterize most members of a given group, having been internalized during the early years as a result of the characteristic mode of socialization. Allowing for idiosyncratic fluctuations, the level of activity-passivity is probably fairly uniform among the members of each cultural group.

[9] Abraham Shumsky, *The Clash of Cultures in Israel* (New York: Teachers College, Columbia University, 1955), pp. 21-22.

At first glance, the cultural differences in level of activity-passivity may seem paradoxical in the light of the previous findings. Earlier in this chapter non-Europeans were reported to be more upward mobile, and now they are found to be more passive although it is the active who tend to be more upward mobile. However, closer consideration shows that this phenomenon is easily explained. Fewer of the non-Europeans are active; among the non-Europeans who are active, however, there is a greater number of upward mobile people than among the active Europeans. This empirical picture emerges most clearly from Table 48. There it may be seen, by observing the number of cases on which the percentages are based, that more Europeans than non-Europeans in each class are classified active. At the same time, however, in observing the upward mobile percentages, it may be seen that non-Europeans are consistently more upward mobile when they are active and when they are passive (except for the first two subgroups—which are too small to be reliable—of lowest-class Europeans). In other words, a minority of the non-Europeans are active; among the group that is active, however, the desire for upward mobility is greater than among the active Europeans. In a sense, the active non-Europeans may be thought of as deviants from their own culture.

In addition to showing the role of the immigrant's cultural background in determining activity-passivity, Table 49 also indicates the effect of education and length of time in Israel on this variable. The higher the level of education, the more likely the immigrant is to be active. Similarly, the longer he is in the country, the greater his tendency to be active. There is also evidence that younger respondents are more active than older ones. All three of these background factors—education, length of time in the country, and age—suggest an increase of activity with the passing of time. Thus it appears that the immigrant's initial level of activity is determined culturally—the Europeans higher, and the non-Europeans lower—but with the passage of time, there is a general increase in the level of activity in both groups. I cannot determine whether the actual rate of change is the same; however, the factors noted operate independently of the immigrant's cultural background.

SUMMARY AND DISCUSSION

This chapter has continued to project the immigrant into his occupational future. Here I have focused on the status of the job to which the immigrant aspires for his son in comparison to the respondent's own job before immigration. It is assumed that immigration inevitably effects a certain measure of occupational change because of differences between the occupational structure of the country of origin and the society into which the immigrant is moving, because of the economic and social dislocation brought about by large-scale immigration, and, in the case of Israel, because of differing value orientations in the occupational sphere.

Aspirations were compared with former occupations, and four categories of immigrants were defined: "upward mobile," "similar status," "downward mobile (idealism)," and "unclassifiable." These categories are relatively defined and in this respect differ from most studies of mobility, which generally focus on movement into absolutely defined, high-ranking occupations.

The first important finding concerns the greater aspirations for upward mobility of the non-European immigrants. In addition, a variable called "activity-passivity" plays an important role in determining occupational aspirations: active people are more upward mobile than passive people. Passive people are more likely to aspire to their own occupation or to one of similar status. Activity-passivity, however, does not condition downward mobility (idealism). It was noted that the definition of activity-passivity bears a strong resemblance to the "getting by" and "getting ahead" concepts of Joseph A. Kahl.

The remainder of the chapter explored the nature of the "activity-passivity" variable. It was found to be an ethnically determined characteristic. European immigrants are more active; the non-Europeans are more passive. The variable was also found to change with time and experience. Activity increases with a higher level of education and with the length of time immigrants have been in Israel, but decreases with age.

These findings seem to indicate that a certain level of activity-passivity may be characteristic of whole cultures, because it has apparently been internalized by most members of the group during the process of socialization. This characteristic operates horizontally among members of the culture group and may be thought of as a basic personality trait. At the same time, certain changes in activity-passivity appear to occur with time or experience, and these changes take place cross-culturally.

The difference in activity-passivity of the two cultural groups conforms to what we know about the over-all cultural patterns of the countries from which the Europeans and non-Europeans have emigrated. Arab countries have traditionally let the old order persist although in recent years the introduction of technology has greatly changed this. Such surface phenomena are a long way, however, from changing the deeply ingrained attitudes and values which have prevailed for generations.[10] In any case, the industrial revolution has come to these countries only recently, whereas it had already changed most parts of Europe during the middle and late nineteenth century. European countries, especially those with Calvinist and capitalistic ethics, are more concerned with doing and changing and improving than are the Arab countries. Jews living in these countries naturally absorbed these cultural patterns and attitudes.

The findings with respect to the upward mobility of the non-Europeans are of particular interest when viewed against the social structure of their countries of origin on one hand and of Israel on the other. The greater upward mobility of the non-Europeans suggests a desire to compensate for the closed social systems which prevailed in the countries from which they emigrated. The release of this need appears to have resulted in a greater aspiration for upward mobility than was expressed by the Europeans. In a relatively open society, the non-Europeans seem to want to take advantage of the opportunities it offers.

At this point it is useful to recall the findings concerning the marked orientation of European immigrants to the professions, and the non-Europeans to the white-collar occupations. The present chapter has pointed to the seeming paradox that non-Euro-

[10] See Margaret Mead, *Cultural Patterns and Technical Change* (New York: Mentor, 1955).

peans are more upward mobile than Europeans. It may be seen that these findings are not a paradox in the light of the relative definition of mobility used here. By this definition an immigrant could be upward mobile and still be aspiring only to medium-status occupations. I believe that this is precisely what occurs among the immigrants observed here. Although more non-Europeans than Europeans tend to be upward mobile in their aspirations, the non-Europeans apparently focus their hopes on occupations of lesser status than Europeans. In other words, non-Europeans aspire more than Europeans to higher-status jobs than they had before immigrating, but they do not aspire so much as the Europeans to the really high-status jobs.

It is of considerable interest to note that many years, often generations, of residence in Arab countries where upward mobility for Jews was very difficult apparently did not cause the Jews in these countries to internalize a norm of immobility. In a society where class lines are stringently observed and occupations are handed down from father to son, it might be expected that the Jews' expectations would be more closely attuned to the social structure. Among the Jewish immigrants observed here, however, a latent desire for mobility seems to have prevailed. Additional research is needed to determine how this desire for mobility structures over time, especially as the non-Europeans become more aware of certain limitations to upward mobility which prevail in Israel.

A final note is in order concerning the need for replication of this type of analysis using different definitions of activity-passivity. Of necessity, the definition used here was unique to the particular situation with which we are dealing. The relative activity or passivity of the individual in other life situations should be used in order to confirm the findings reported.

Five · Closing

11 · Conclusions

The study has focused on attitude and behavior patterns of immigrants during their first year in Israel. The data were collected in 1949 and 1950 while the newcomers were still living in the temporary transit camps; very few had been in Israel for longer than a year. The fundamental issue was, thus, the earliest reactions to the society into which the immigrant was moving. The processes under observation were those that preceded actual entry into the Israeli social system.

The study was divided into three parts: response to the strain of transit, first gropings at acculturation, and orientation toward the future.

ETHNIC PATTERNS

Before proceeding to a summary of the various substantive problems considered in the study, I must note a number of cross-cutting observations which run through much of the material. The major conclusions of the study will be presented on a horizontal level, grouping the findings on each of the substantive problems considered. Here I shall discuss some findings on a vertical level in an attempt to draw together certain threads which run throughout the study and are major themes in the interpretation. These findings concern the various patterns of ethnic behavior and the interpretive framework which was repeatedly used in their analysis.

One of the most striking impressions to emerge from the study is the generally high salience of the ethnic group during the period under discussion. There was hardly a problem in which differential ethnic patterns of attitude and behavior did not emerge despite the fact that I was unable to observe in detail all the ethnic groups in our population and had to use a gross classification of the population into Europeans and non-Europeans.

Since the immigrants under observation had been in Israel for such a brief time, the differences observed between the two ethnic groups were largely attributed to differences in background and social structure in the countries of origin. With time, the Europeans and non-Europeans undoubtedly will come to occupy differential positions in the Israeli social structure as well; however, in the situation of the temporary transit camp, we have interpreted the past factors to be more salient than the position of the ethnic groups in the local social system. In the present set of data, the past factors are more impressionistic than systematic. They represent elements of social structure which have been used here to aid in interpreting certain observed empirical phenomena; because they refer to conditions in the countries of origin, they could not, in the present framework, be directly examined.

Three elements in the social structure of the countries of origin account separately and/or jointly for most of the differences in ethnic attitude and behavior patterns observed. These elements are (1) the differential social and economic conditions, which resulted in differing levels of relative deprivation once the immigrant was in Israel, (2) the religious-secular balance of the culture of the Jewish populations before immigrating, and (3) the degree of social mobility possible for Jews.

By and large, the non-European countries had lower standards of living and sociocultural levels than the European countries; this is linked to the late arrival of the industrial revolution, the dominant religious culture, and the very late appearance of nationalism and political democracy. Important from the present point of view are the different expectations induced by the various backgrounds in immigrants arriving in Israel from European and non-European countries. By and large, it has been assumed that these differential expectations help account for the higher level of morale among the non-Europeans and for their markedly more favorable over-all reaction to Israel. In particular, ethnic origin was used in interpreting the approach and withdrawal patterns in acculturation.

On the whole, it was assumed in the analysis that the Jewish communities in the non-European countries of origin were characterized by traditional religious culture that had few elements of secularism. In the European countries, on the other hand, the balance was much more heavily on the secular side. There were, of course, strong religious elements in the European Jewish population; however, there was a considerable number of non-traditional, secularly oriented Jews. In Europe, the general cultural ethic, which undoubtedly played a large part in orienting the Jewish population, was more secular. In the non-European countries, not only was a traditional religious orientation more widespread among the Jews, but the dominant Moslem culture was also strongly religious and generally reinforced the religious frame of reference.

The religious-secular balance was introduced to explain the differential role played by Zionist ideology among the European and non-European immigrants. For the Europeans, the ideology served somewhat as a kind of insulation, protecting them against frustration with the reality of Israel. For the non-Europeans, among whom the Zionist movement had also functioned in the countries of origin, the ideology played no role insofar as insulation against frustration and disappointment is concerned. On the whole, the non-Europeans were also found to be less disappointed with the reality of Israel, regardless of whether they had a Zionist ideological commitment. The interpretation suggested that the traditional religious orientation of the non-European immigrants was basically so positive to Israel that the Zionist movement had little to offer its members beyond the orientation they had acquired from their traditional culture. Since the Zionist movement in the non-European countries was able to offer only a Zionist religious orientation (a secular ideology would have been generally unacceptable), it added little to the prevalent religious frame of reference which had always included certain Messianic elements as well as a generally positive orientation to the Holy Land. In the generally secular European countries, the Zionist movement assumed the role of a political ideology even though some segments of it had a religious emphasis. Thus commitment to the ideology entailed a markedly different orientation to Israel and its problems from non-commitment; the basically secular nature of the culture in which the movement functioned made possible a clear distinction between adherents and non-adherents. It is in this general context that the insulating role of the ideology for the Europeans becomes meaningful; it apparently provided a frame of reference from which the immigrant was able to categorize seemingly frustrating experiences to collective values and long-range goals so that they were not frustrating to him. The non-Zionist immigrant was less able to do this.

In general, the non-European countries were described as considerably less socially mobile than the European countries; in particular, the opportunities for Jews to rise in the occupational and status system were much more severely limited. Even under conditions of extreme anti-Semitism, the barriers to social mobility were seldom institutionalized in Europe as they were in the Moslem countries. In many of the Moslem societies, the Jewish population had lived for generations under conditions of oppression and semi-servitude. These countries were untouched by the industrial revolution and by Western concepts of democracy until recently, so that their social systems as a whole were less open. However, the position of the Jewish population was, more often than not, especially depressed and institutionalized on that level by the authorities.

This third element of social structure—the differing opportunities for social mobility—was used to help explain the different attitudes toward social mobility on the part of European and non-European immigrants. In particular, the non-Europeans were thought to be compensating, in a certain sense, for their former lack of social mobility by fairly strong efforts in that direction once they were in Israel. This factor was also used to interpret the findings concerning status strivings as expressed by occupational aspirations and the over-all patterns of acculturation observed among the Europeans and the non-Europeans.

STRAIN

In Part One, certain factors in the immigrant's make-up were examined for their roles in conditioning his response to the strain inherent in the transit situation. It is the strain of transit which more or less sets the stage for our analysis. Since it is one of the dominant themes, I shall recapitulate the elements which make up the structural strain of the transit situation.

The Strain of Transit

The first and basic element of strain is the fundamental ambiguity and lack of structure for the new immigrant in the transit situation. He was faced with problems the solution of which was crucial to his welfare, yet he lacked adequate means to solve them. This lack was brought about partially by his newness in the society. Its norms and institutions were not sufficiently known to him to allow him to attain certain basic goals. Often norms which had been appropriate in his country of origin were abandoned, either because the immigrant rejected former cultural values or because he sensed the values were inappropriate to the solution of problems in the Israeli value and institutional systems. One of the most severe problems faced by all immigrants in this unstructured context was that of coming to some decision concerning future plans for settlement, work, and housing. The combination of the unstructured situation and the pressure to come to some decisions created a basic situation of strain.

Three other situational factors contributed to strain during the transit period. One of these was the widespread unemployment of the immigrant population. The economic system had not adjusted to the absorption of a mass influx of immigrants, and the result was that some 70 per cent of the men were unemployed. There was also a widespread feeling among immigrants that one of the public institutions would and should, as a matter of right, assist them financially or otherwise in their settlement problems. Despite the best intentions, however, the means for such assistance were severely limited, and a large number of immigrants did not receive any help. In such a setting, failure to obtain assistance was another major source of strain. The final situational factor was the prolonged stay in the immigrant transit camp. The physical and social conditions of the camp were inherently difficult; there were crowding, lack of privacy, public eating facilities, inadequate sanitary accommodations, overworked bureaucrats in positions of authority, isolation from the mainstream of Israeli social life. If these factors initially set up a difficult situation, the strain inherent in the situation increased as the immigrant remained in the camp. As the name implies, the transit camps were originally planned to house the immigrants for a temporary period until more permanent accommodations could be arranged. However, the social and economic problems of absorbing a mass influx of immigrants were exceedingly great, and housing for immigrants constituted one of the major problems. At the time of this study, some of the immigrants had been living in a transit camp for as long as a year.

On an attitudinal level there were also elements conducive to strain in the immigrants' situation. The most important of these is the immigrant's frustration with the reality of Israel. People whose expectations of Israel were markedly higher than what they found would be more likely to be under strain than people whose expectations had been more realistic. Another attitudinal factor that operates on the level of perception and internal system balance is the immigrant's feeling of well-being in his family. This is a more general problem, but one that is heightened by the transit camp situation, which has certain structural barriers to normal family life. This was particularly true of immigrants whose traditional extended-family group broke down because of the vicissitudes of immigration or the conditions of housing in the transit camp.

Response to Strain

Two elements in the immigrant's past frame of reference were examined for their role in conditioning his response to various aspects of the over-all strain situation described. One of these was positive—the immigrant's commitment to Zionist ideology and his identification with the goals and values of Israel. The other is negative—the experience for immigrants of European origin of life in a Nazi concentration camp. In addition, I chose to examine the reference groups which play a role in conditioning the immigrant's response to the strain of unemployment.

In a general sense, it may be said that both of the factors in the immigrant's past play what may be termed a "constructive" role in helping him meet the strain of the transit situation. This is particularly interesting in view of the fact that the Nazi concentration camp was an extremely negative experience involving a major trauma. Nevertheless, the experience of internment by the Nazis and of a Zionist ideological commitment generally assisted the immigrant in overcoming the strain to which he was subject during his early period in Israel.

Ideology as Organizer

The role of ideological commitment was examined with reference to two types of strain: (1) the need for decision-making concerning plans for eventual settlement and (2) initial disappointment with Israel. With respect to the first type of strain, it was found that an ideological commitment plays a constructive role in making it possible for the immigrant to use available information to come to some decision concerning his settlement problems. The positive role of the ideological commitment is made even more graphic by the parallel finding that immigrants without such a commitment find the same information resources dysfunctional. For uncommitted people, additional information about the country, its institutions, and its norms increases the strain of decision-making by intensifying their uncertainty. An ideological frame of reference apparently provides a framework into which the immigrant fits pieces of information in a functional way.

Such a finding points to both theoretical and applied conclusions. On a theoretical level, it demonstrates the role of a predisposing frame of reference in using information resources for problem-solving. This role is, perhaps, less striking than the finding that the absence of such a frame of reference results in a dysfunctional use of information in a problem-solving situation.

On an applied level, this finding carries implications on many fronts—education, communication, propaganda, and the general area of decision-making. In all of these fields, it is clear from the present finding that communication in an unstructured field is likely to be unsatisfactory. For communication to be effective in the sense that it is picked up by the recipient and, on a more complex level, used by the recipient, it must be directed toward a field of perception which is organized within a meaningful frame of reference. Before communication can be effective, the communicator must be concerned with his audience's predisposing frame of reference.

Ideology as Insulation

With regard to the other problem of strain—frustration with Israel—ideological commitment also played a constructive role, although not for the entire population. It was found that the cultural context in which ideological commitment was acquired is important in determining whether it will play an active role in conditioning the immigrant's disappointment with Israel. Thus it was found that, for immigrants of European origin, ideological commitment acts somewhat as an insulation against frustration. Those who had been active members of a Zionist group before immigrating tended to be less disappointed with Israel than those who had not been active Zionists. For the Europeans, the ideology apparently provided a certain perspective which made otherwise frustrating experiences in the new country relatively unfrustrating, possibly because they were made meaningful in the context of the Zionist ideology. For this reason, the role of the ideology for this ethnic group has been termed an "insulating" one; it protects against disappointment. For the non-European immigrants, however, the ideology did not play a role in conditioning disappointment with the country; active Zionists among them were no more or less frustrated with Israel than non-Zionists.

This finding points to the importance of the cultural differences between the two groups in determining the meaning of an ideological commitment. An ideological commitment is related to the social structure and value systems of the different ethnic communities and to the place of the Zionist movement in that context. As already noted, in the European countries the Zionist movement functioned largely in a secular, political frame of reference, whereas in the non-European countries it assumed more of a religious, Messianic theme. Needless to say, this was not an all-or-none proposition, but only a general tendency. However, since Jews in the non-European countries lived in a traditional, religious subculture, it may be suggested that the context and doctrine of the organized Zionist movement were not too different from the one that was prevalent among the unorganized segments of the population. The important point is that among the non-Europeans, the Zionist movement apparently did not offer a very different basis for orientation to Israel than the one that was already prevalent among the unorganized immigrants. This impression is further confirmed by the finding that non-Europeans as a whole are also less disappointed than Europeans with Israel as they found it. Thus, the traditional, religious culture provided a positive orientation to Israel, and this orientation was a function of the over-all culture, not of experience in the Zionist movement. The European immigrant acquired a different orientation to Israel. My suggestion would be that this cleavage is a function of the generally secular nature of the Zionist movement in Europe and of the greater political significance of the ideology in Western culture. To be or not to be a Zionist in Europe implied considerably greater differences in orientation to Israel than it did in non-European countries.

At the same time, this finding, as well as the one concerning the functional role of the ideology in using information and the one concerning the repercussions of frustration among those with and without an ideological commitment, applies to the non-European population as well as to the European. Thus, it would be incorrect to assume that the ideology plays no role among the non-Europeans even though it does not insulate the immigrant against frustration. It still provides a meaningful frame of reference by which information is so organized that it can be useful in aiding the immigrant to make plans for more permanent settlement. It also implies a certain emotional investment in Israel. The over-all orientation of the Zionist and the non-Zionist among the non-Europeans cannot, therefore, be considered identical.

Ideology and Frustration

Another finding on this subject points to the somewhat less constructive role of the ideology in assisting the immigrant to weather the strain of transition. This finding is associated with the apparent affective implications of the ideology for the immigrant; thus there is evidence that, when immigrants are disappointed with Israel, this frustration tends to have more serious emotional repercussions for people with an ideological commitment than it has for people without such a commitment. The data indicate greater psychosomatic disturbances and somewhat greater displacement of frustration among disappointed Zionists than among disappointed non-Zionists. This is true for Europeans and non-Europeans. The picture is not altogether consistent on several of the empirical variables examined with respect to displacement of frustration; however, there is sufficient evidence to suggest that such frustration is a greater emotional shock to Zionists, who apparently have a greater affective investment in Israel and in their own expectations regarding it.

The Nazi Concentration Camp and Hardening

The experience of internment in a Nazi concentration camp, although a traumatic event in the individual's life, also acts, in a certain sense, to assist the immigrant in overcoming the early strain of the transit situation. The process by which this assistance takes place has been termed "hardening" to new strain in that the trauma of the Nazi concentration camp hardens the individual so that he is better able to withstand new strain of a fairly minor variety. Thus, although the experience of the concentration camp was a negative one, the evidence here points to a kind of positive aftereffect in the sense of assisting the individual to weather additional strain.

Also, under fairly favorable conditions, concentration camp survivors tend to be more pessimistic about their future in Israel than a control population. When viewed with the finding concerning hardening, the behavior of the concentration camp survivors appears to be more rigid with regard to the future than that of immigrants who have not undergone this traumatic experience. When subject to additional current strain, however, the level of their optimism shifts very little.

Reference Groups and Unemployment

In observing response to the strain of unemployment, it was assumed that, among other factors, this response would be a function of the immigrant's comparison of his own employment status with the employment status prevalent in the reference groups which are salient in that context. Thus in cases in which the individual's employment status is better than that of the group to which he refers, his morale will be high; in cases in which his employment status is worse than that of the group to which he refers, his morale will be low. It is the comparison which determines response to the strain of unemployment.

When the transit camps were divided into two categories—those with high unemployment and those with low unemployment—it was found that these ecological settings do impart reference norms against which the individual evaluates his own employment status. Thus, employed immigrants living in camps where unemployment was generally high indicated the highest level of morale. Conversely, unemployed immigrants living in camps where unemployment was relatively low showed the lowest level of morale.

Although morale was generally reduced by unemployment, the findings indicate that expectations play an important role in determining how much it was reduced. Thus unemployment does not reduce morale very much when the expected thing is unemployment. However, when one's group norm indicates employment to be the rule, unemployment leads to low morale.

A norm of employment in one's reference group also functions to increase one's expectations about the quality of employment. During a period of widespread unemployment, the immigrants who were fortunate enough to find employment generally did not get very remunerative or high-status jobs. Among the immigrants who did get jobs, those living in camps with a relatively low rate of unemployment appeared to feel somewhat dissatisfied with their jobs, for their morale was found to be lower than that of employed immigrants living in camp with more widespread unemployment.

ACCULTURATION

Acculturation was investigated over a year-long period by examining the individual's tendency to accept certain ideal norms of the new society, by observing the dominant sources of advice and information to which he turns, and by noting his perception of hostility or friendliness in the receiving society as the year progresses.

The data indicate two dominant patterns of acculturation. For the Europeans, a pattern of withdrawal was characteristic; for the non-Europeans, a pattern of approach. This means that during the first year in Israel, the European immigrants, living in the temporary transit camps, tend to reject the norms of the new society more as the year progresses; they also rely more on other immigrants as sources of advice and information and perceive increasing hostility in the host population. The non-Europeans, on the other hand, show a reverse pattern—they tend to accept certain ideal norms of the new society more as the year progresses, they rely increasingly on old-timers in the population as sources of advice and information, and they perceive increased friendliness in the receiving population.

These over-all patterns were found to be partially a function of the different levels of morale characterizing the two ethnic groups. Europeans, when examined on six morale variables, are consistently more depressed with Israel than are non-Europeans. Furthermore, the evidence indicates a fairly clear relationship between morale and the pattern of approach or withdrawal; on the whole, the higher morale, the more likely a pattern of approach; the lower morale, the more likely a pattern of withdrawal. At the same time, the relationship between the two sets of variables is far from perfect, and morale cannot be said to provide a complete explanation for approach and withdrawal. Thus, withdrawal often appears among Europeans with high morale as well as among those with low morale; conversely, approach is found among non-Europeans with low as well as among those with high morale. I am unable to propose a complete and testable explanation for these phenomena and can only offer a number of *post hoc* theories which should be tested systematically in later research on this topic.

It was suggested that relative deprivation might be operating in the context described. This would account for the differential response of European and non-European immigrants to conditions in Israel when viewed against the social and economic conditions to which they had been accustomed in their countries of origin. The Europeans, who generally came from more favorable social and economic surroundings, found the transit camp situation increasingly difficult as the year wore on. The non-Europeans, on the other hand, judged the local situation by less favorable standards of comparison. The result was that, on the whole, their reaction to Israel was considerably more favorable. This theory proposes that relative deprivation more or less sets the stage for the immigrant's initial reaction to Israel and that subsequent experiences continue to operate in the initial framework. Thus the Europeans, for whom the transit camp was apparently a severe disappointment and trial compared to the conditions to which they had been accustomed, may have hoped when they first arrived that these conditions would improve with time. When little change occurred during their first year, their general depression increased, bringing in its wake the growing pattern of withdrawal from the new society. The non-Europeans, who were generally less negatively impressed with the initial conditions they met in Israel, became, with time, more-or-less reconciled to the transit camps. There is impressionistic evidence that they even developed a fairly intensive social life among themselves on a family or national-origin basis. For them, therefore, the conditions did not become markedly worse with time. Since they were able to establish some sort of framework for a traditional social life, it may even, in a certain sense, have improved over the year.

It remains to propose some explanation for the Europeans with relatively high morale who nevertheless display the characteristic withdrawal pattern. Relative deprivation provides a helpful theory only for the group in which withdrawal may be considered a function of low morale. For the other European immigrants, it appears that withdrawal is a function of some other variable which is not associated with their morale. They are characterized by a fairly high level of morale; yet they withdraw increasingly from Israel during the first year they are there. It may be suggested that the prevailing norms and institutional structure of Israeli society are not to their liking and that they are oriented to another value system. They seem to like the new society and its values less as time goes on and association with it increases; perhaps their orientation to another system of values is reinforced. At first glance, however, the apparent separation of the orientation to Israel and the level of morale seems paradoxical.

In addition to relative deprivation, there seem to be certain other factors motivating the pattern of approach observed among the non-Europeans. These function over and above the morale-acculturation configuration. In particular, they are associated with certain elements in the social structure of the non-European countries of origin.

The first of these factors concerns the opportunities for social mobility among Jews in the non-European countries. By and large, such opportunities were limited. However, a long history of living in such closed societies apparently did not diminish the desire for social mobility among the Jews in these countries. Upon arrival in Israel, one of the earliest expressions of their desire for social mobility was the pattern of approach to Israel. One way for immigrants to get ahead in a new society is to accept its ideal norms, to try to rely on the old-time population for advice and information, and to perceive a large measure of friendliness on the part of the receiving population. The desire for mobility motivated a need for relatively quick entry into the new social structure. The period under study was probably too early for the non-Europeans to have had time to sense certain structural barriers to full social mobility which undoubtedly existed to some extent in the new society.

Another factor which is associated with the desire for mobility is the motivation of non-Europeans to identify with the Western and European segments of the population. This need grows not only from an instrumental point of view, which sees such identification as an effective means of mobility, but also from certain feelings of inferiority about their own cultures. The latter feeling may have been brought from the non-European countries of origin, where technological progress and cultural superiority were traditionally associated with the Western elements of the population. It was probably reinforced in Israel by the cultural emphasis on Western values and norms of behavior. The non-Europeans found themselves in a society where Western patterns were associated with the groups in power. This situation may have reinforced whatever feelings of inferiority the immigrants brought with them and stimulated a desire to identify with the Western segments of the new society. One way of accomplishing this is to approach all the society's norms, rely on the old-time community, and make every effort to enter the social structure.

A final motivating element in the approach pattern of the

non-Europeans concerns the heightened level of their Jewish identification. The non-Europeans were characterized by a more traditional, religious orientation to Israel, which often expressed itself in a semi-Messianic reference about the re-establishment of the state. This is not to say that there were no religious European immigrants; among the Europeans, however, they constituted only a segment of the population, whereas among the non-Europeans a traditional, religious orientation was almost universal. In addition, among the Europeans the religious groups were often highly critical of the basically secular nature of the Israeli community, whereas among the non-Europeans—possibly because of a less sophisticated outlook, possibly because of the Messianic element in their religious frame of reference—the religious tradition seemed to provide an over-all positive orientation to the country.

ORIENTATION TOWARD THE FUTURE

The immigrant's orientation toward the future was examined in terms of his occupational aspirations and how he views entry into the Israeli occupational system. In order to avoid the possible effect of unemployment on the free expression of such aspirations, the immigrant's aspirations for his son's future occupation were used as the data for occupational aspirations.

One major finding concerns ethnic patterns of occupational aspirations. Europeans are more oriented to the professions; non-Europeans tend to focus on white-collar jobs. It was suggested that this finding could be associated with the relative opportunities for mobility open to Jews in the various countries of origin. The non-European immigrants were socialized in an environment in which access to high-status occupations was limited for them. They may, therefore, despite a desire to rise in the social scale, have focused on somewhat lower-ranking occupations of the sort that were generally open to them. These occupations are government posts, teaching, and various white-collar jobs. In view of the opportunities offered by their countries of origin, these jobs may reflect relatively high aspirations for the non-Europeans. In addition, it is possible that, despite the relatively short time they have been in Israel, the non-European immigrants have somehow sensed the barriers to completely free mobility and have revised their aspirations accordingly.

Mobility was determined by a comparison of the local status of the job the immigrant aspired to for his son with the immigrant's job in his country of origin. By means of this comparison, immigrants were divided into four categories: "upward mobile," "similar status," "downward mobile (idealism)," and "unclassifiable." Downward mobile (idealism) carries a unique meaning because of the Israeli pioneering ethic.

Non-European immigrants are more upward mobile in their aspirations than European immigrants. This finding may result from a desire to compensate for years of living in a social system that was socially immobile, particularly for Jews.

One of the most interesting findings concerns the role of a variable termed "activity-passivity" in conditioning occupational aspirations. This variable concerned the extent to which the immigrant accepted his over-all situation or felt an obligation to assume a more positive role in directing it. People defined as "active" are more upward mobile than people defined as "passive." The active are also less likely to aspire to their own status level, but are no different from the passive in downward mobility.

In examining the "activity-passivity" variable, it was found to be an ethnically determined characteristic. On the whole, Europeans tend to be more active and non-Europeans more passive. A given level of "activity-passivity" seems to be typical of each ethnic group. In a sense, then, this variable may be considered a basic personality trait in the sense used by Kardiner: it is apparently internalized on a similar level by all members of the ethnic group during the early stages of socialization.[1]

The behavior of the non-Europeans in this context deserves some special clarification. The findings about their attitudes toward mobility appear, at first glance, to be paradoxical: they are more upward mobile than the Europeans, but also they are

[1] Abram Kardiner, *The Individual and his Society* (New York: Columbia University Press, 1939).

frequently less active. Apparently, the minority of non-Europeans who deviate from their ethnic norm are more upward mobile than the active Europeans, for whom activity is an accepted attitude. Deviance from the norm apparently causes the non-Europeans to express their activity in a stronger desire for upward mobility.

It is useful to consider the findings just reported in conjunction with the data on the status of occupations to which immigrants aspire for their sons. It was stated that non-Europeans focus on white-collar jobs whereas Europeans tend to choose the highest-ranking professions. Here I have just reported that non-Europeans are more upward mobile than Europeans. The latter finding seems, therefore, to mean that, despite a desire for upward mobility, non-Europeans do not focus on really high-status occupations. They seem to desire a higher occupational rank for their sons than they themselves occupied in their country of origin; they do not, however, aim at the highest occupational ranks in the society.

Appendix A · The Questionnaire

MAJOR SCALE AREAS AND
OVER-ALL FREQUENCY DISTRIBUTIONS

As many attitudes as possible were defined as Guttman scales. In all cases described below, reproducibility of the scale was over .90. The foldover technique was used to determine an intensity function, and the zero point of the intensity function used to dichotomize most variables for purposes of analysis. Except when indicated, reference to one segment of the scale continuum refers to a cutting point determined by the zero point.[1]

In addition to the scales, there were several single items used in the analysis. These are described in the relevant chapters. Background data on each respondent were collected, but will not here be described in detail since the relevant variables are described in the text.

[1] Stouffer *et al.*, *Measurement* . . . , *op. cit.*, chaps 3–7.

The questionnaire had six major substantive sections. The scales and other additional items in each, as well as the over-all distribution of the population on each major variable, will be presented. The grouping of variables presented here does not correspond to the organization of the substantive problems analyzed in the body of the study because the substantive problems require a variety of variables in different groupings for the specific purposes of analysis. Thus, any empirical variable may be used in a number of chapters dealing with differing aspects of immigrant behavior. The six groupings listed here are essentially a heuristic device for convenience of presentation.

OCCUPATIONAL PROBLEMS

The first occupational problem concerned the extent of the immigrant's decisiveness with respect to making any plans for getting a job. This area probed the uncertainty of the immigrant's occupational plans without entering into specific occupational choices. The items in "decisiveness of plans for settlement" were as follows:

Do you have any definite plans concerning what you will do here in Israel?

Do you feel your plans are practical?

Do you think you'll be able to carry out your plans?

Do you have any definite ideas about arrangements for housing? For a job?

The data indicated that approximately half (53 per cent) the immigrant population had no decisive plans for settlement.

The more specific occupational problems were intentions with respect to two occupations in which the settlement authorities had a special interest—agriculture and shopkeeping. Immigrants were also asked about their attitudes toward supplementary farming on a plot of land to be provided near their home if agriculture was not to be their full-time occupation. In addition, they were asked whether they had received any information about the possibilities of farming as a gainful occupation.

The items in "attitude toward agriculture" were as follows:

Would you like to be a farmer?

Do you feel that you could make a satisfactory living as a farmer?

Do you like work on the soil?

Do you feel that you are personally suited to be a farmer?

One third (34 per cent) indicated that they would favor agriculture as an occupation.

The items in "attitude toward shopkeeping" were as follows:

Are you interested in registering to obtain a shop or kiosk? (Certain immigrants, notably social welfare cases, were eligible to receive shops and had to register for that privilege.)

Do you think you could make a satisfactory living from a store or kiosk?

Do you think that there is too much competition in shopkeeping?

Do you feel that you have enough business experience to succeed as a shopkeeper?

Sixty per cent expressed a preference for shopkeeping.

The items in "attitude toward supplementary farming" were as follows:

Would you like to receive a plot of land next to your home for supplementary farming (truck farming, poultry run, and the like)?

Do you think you will actually be able to cultivate such a plot of land?

197

Do you think you will have sufficient time and energy to develop the plot?

Are you prepared for the risks involved in farming?

Two thirds (65 per cent) favored supplementary farming near their home provided that they were primarily engaged in another occupation.

The items in "information received concerning farming" were as follows:

Did you ever receive any explanation of the conditions under which immigrants can settle as farmers?

Have you heard any lectures on agricultural settlement?

Have you been told that, if you decide on farming as your occupation, you will receive special assistance?

Did anyone try to convince you to become a farmer?

Seventeen per cent of the immigrants reported having received information about the benefits offered to those who chose farming as their occupation.

Some additional information on occupational attitudes of immigrants was obtained from a question asking what occupation the respondent would like his son to enter. This question involved some problems that are rather different from those discussed in the specific occupational plans presented thus far; it concerns aspirations for social and occupational mobility.

STRUCTURE OF SOCIAL RELATIONS IN THE TRANSIT CAMP

There were four groups of questions in the section of the questionnaire that asked about social relations. The first group concerned family relations and the following attitude areas: "family solidarity," "family tension," and "tension in relationships with children."

The items on "family solidarity" were as follows:

If you had another free hour during the day, with whom would you like to spend it? (With family, with friends, alone?)

Would you like to spend more time with your immediate family?

Does your family eat together on Saturday or on Friday night?

Would you say the relations among members of your immediate family are good?

Eighteen per cent reported low family solidarity.

The items on "family tension" were as follows:

Would you say there is more or less tension between you and your wife/husband than there was before you immigrated?

Do you find that your wife/husband is more irritable than she/he was before you immigrated?

Would you say your wife/husband is as considerate of your needs and feelings as she/he was before you immigrated?

Do you feel that the difficulties which your family has met in immigration and resettlement have caused you to increase your esteem for your wife/husband?

The above items defined a Guttman quasi-scale, and the population was divided into three groups. The intensity function was not used to dichotomize this scale because of the large concentration of subjects in a middle score indicating "no difference." It was therefore decided to trichotomize the continuum, using the scores on either side of "no difference" to indicate "tension" and "no tension"; the "no-difference" score was the middle group. Eleven per cent of the sample fell into the tension-between-husband-and-wife group.

The items on "tension in relationships with children" were as follows:

Do you find that your children disturb you more than they used to before you immigrated?

Do you find that your children are more irritating than before you immigrated?

Do your children show as much respect for you as they used to before you immigrated?

Are the children as obedient as they used to be before you immigrated?

Nineteen per cent reported tension in relationships with children.

It is of some interest to note that the number of "no answers" was disproportionately large in the three areas described above, giving reason to suspect that the tension might well be greater than reported. The number of "no answers" on each of the three areas in family relations in the transit camp was as follows: family solidarity, 163; family tension, 503; tension in relationships with children, 739.

The second set of questions concerned "social relationships with neighbors" in the transit camp. Attitude areas in this group were as follows: "perception of neighborly friendliness," "neighbor solidarity," "perception of general hostility in the camp," and "community participation."

The items on "perception of neighborly friendliness" were as follows:

In case of sudden need, do you think your neighbors would help you?

Do your neighbors quarrel with you?

Do you think your neighbors would lend you money should the need arise?

Fifty-three per cent of the immigrants perceived their neighbors in the transit camp to be friendly.

The items on "neighbor solidarity" were as follows:

Do you ever borrow anything, such as food, household goods, clothing, from your neighbors?

Have your neighbors ever helped you with anything around your quarters?

Do you visit your neighbors?

Do the neighbors ever visit you?

Forty-two per cent indicated a feeling of solidarity.

The scale on "perception of hostility in neighborhood" required respondents to state the extent of their agreement with the following statements:

There are a lot of thefts in this neighborhood.

People often try to take things from me by force in this neighborhood.

You can only get along by strong-arm methods around here.

This neighborhood has a bad influence on children.

Seventy-six per cent stated they did not feel hostility in the atmosphere of the transit camp.

The items on "community participation" were as follows:

Are you active in the local committee which is supposed to deal with immigrants' needs?

Did you vote in the camp elections?

Do you attend community meetings?

Do you generally like to take part in public committees which deal with communal matters?

Twenty-five per cent of the immigrants reported that they took some role in community activities.

A third group of questions related to "use of the mass media" and asked about newspaper reading; radio listening; movie, theater, and lecture attendance. All of the items in this section were single questions, not scales. Cutting points were determined arbitrarily by the frequency distribution of the different categories of replies.

A final set of questions concerned "immigrants' general attitude toward the transit camp." The object was to observe the extent to which the immigrants accepted or rejected the camp situation. Two areas were investigated—"attitudes toward the Jewish Agency officials," who ran the camps, and "general acceptance of the camp situation."

The items on "attitude toward the Jewish Agency officials" were as follows:

Do you think the Jewish Agency officials are really trying to help you?

Do you feel that the Jewish Agency officials understand your problems?

Do the Jewish Agency officials seriously consider your personal point of view?

In general, are the Jewish Agency officials successful in carrying out their jobs?

Seventy-one per cent of the immigrants had a generally favorable attitude toward the Jewish Agency officials. It is likely that, for a variety of reasons, many were unwilling to express open dissatisfaction.

The items on "general acceptance of the camp situation" were as follows:

Are you in a hurry to get out of this camp?

Do you really mind if you have to spend a little more time in this camp?

Are you making any effort to move out of the camp?

Have you made any effort to find work and housing outside the camp?

Sixty per cent of the respondents more or less accepted the camp situation.

MORALE

Six aspects of the immigrants' morale were investigated. "Orientation toward the future" attempted to assess the respondent's feeling of optimism or pessimism about his future in Israel. "Personal adjustment" probed the respondent's feeling of well-being and security. "Disappointment with Israel" asked a series of questions concerning the immigrant's reaction to the reality of the new country in comparison to the expectations he had before immigrating. "Desire to emigrate" investigated the extent of the newly arrived immigrant's feelings of alienation and the possibility of his leaving Israel and moving to another country. "Feelings of exploitation" concerned the immigrant's feeling that people are taking advantage of him because of his status as a new immigrant who is unfamiliar with his surroundings. Finally, a quasi-scale of "psychosomatic disturbances" attempted to assess the individual's emotional stability as indicated by somatic upsets.

The items on "orientation toward the future" were as follows:

Do you think there is a good chance that you will get settled in the near future?

Do you think things will improve for you in the coming years?

Do you think you will be happy in Israel?

Do you think conditions in Israel will improve with time?

Three quarters (74 per cent) of the immigrants indicated a positive orientation toward the future.

The items on "personal adjustment" were as follows:

In general, are you in good spirits?

Do you feel worried and confused?

Do you think your luck is worse than most other people's?

Are you occasionally so pessimistic that you feel nothing is worth-while?

Do you think you'll be able to adjust to conditions in Israel?

Eighty-nine per cent reported positive personal adjustment.

The items on "disappointment with Israel" were as follows:

In comparison to your hopes before immigration, what sort of an impression does Israel make on you now?

Have you been disappointed in what you have seen of Israel?

Are conditions more or less difficult than what you had been led to expect?

Sixty-five per cent of the immigrants said they were not generally disappointed with Israel.

The items on "desire to emigrate" were as follows:

Do you want to leave Israel?

Would you prefer to live in another country?

Have you considered the possibilities of settling in another country?

If you received assistance to emigrate to America or Australia (or to some other country), would you want to move there?

Sixteen per cent indicated some interest in emigration.

The items on "feelings of exploitation" required the respondent to state the extent of his agreement with the following statements:

You have to be careful here because people generally give you less than what is really coming to you.

People try to take advantage of us because we're new in the country.

I don't feel that people around here are fair.

Immigrants have a particularly hard time here because everyone tries to exploit them.

Sixty-nine per cent did not feel particularly exploited.

The items used in the quasi-scale "psychosomatic disturbances" were the same as those used by the United States Army in World War II.[2] Thirty-five per cent of the immigrants reported no psychosomatic disturbances.

ATTITUDE TOWARD THE HOST SOCIETY

One problem investigated concerns "attitudes toward the government," specifically its efforts in helping immigrants.

The items in "attitude toward the government" were as follows:

Do you think the government is doing everything possible to help settle the immigrants?

Do you think the government is really concerned with the fate of the immigrants?

Some people say the government is doing nothing to help the immigrants. Do you agree?

Do you think another government would help the immigrants more?

Ninety-two per cent of the immigrants reported a positive attitude toward the government and its efforts on their behalf. It is difficult to say whether such an overwhelmingly positive attitude is

[2] *Ibid.*, pp. 536–538.

the result of fear of expressing unfavorable sentiments toward the government or whether it reflects real appreciation for the government's efforts on behalf of immigrants. However, the former possibility seems more likely.

The items included in a second area entitled "perception of friendliness on the part of the host society" were as follows:

What is your general impression of the old-time Israelis?

Do you think the old-timers try to help newly arrived immigrants?

In general, do the old-timers understand the problems facing immigrants?

Are the old-timers particularly concerned about the future of the immigrants?

Two thirds (67 per cent) perceived friendliness.

A final area in this section relates to the immigrants' major "sources of advice and information." The items in "sources of advice and information" were as follows:

When you need advice on a personal matter, whom do you prefer to turn to for advice, a new immigrant or an old-time Israeli?

Among the immigrants you know, are there many with enough knowledge and understanding to give you useful advice?

In general, would you depend more on information received from an immigrant or from an old-time Israeli?

Do you think that immigrants have a better understanding of one another's problems than do old-time Israelis?

Sixty-six per cent of the immigrants would prefer to rely on old-time Israelis as their major source of advice and information.

ACCULTURATION

Four norms representing several goals and ideal values of the Israeli social system were selected, and the attitudes of the population toward them were observed. These were "attitude toward urban living," "collective versus individual orientation," "attitude toward free immigration," and "attitude toward ethnically mixed housing."

The items in "attitude toward urban living" were as follows:

Do you prefer to live in the city or in the country?

If you were in a position to choose between living in the city and living in a rural settlement, which would you choose?

Do you feel that city life has many advantages over village life?

Seventy-five per cent of the immigrants favored urban living.

The items in "collective versus individual orientation" required the respondent to indicate which of the values in the following pairs was more important to him:

Security in a job or a feeling that his job is helping constructively to build the country.

A high-status position among the workers or a feeling of building something.

A central location or a place that is in need of settlers.

A quiet, pleasant location or a place that is short of workers.

Forty-three per cent are defined collectively oriented by this scale.

The items in "attitude toward free immigration" were as follows:

Do you feel that too many immigrants are coming to Israel at one time?

Do you think that immigration should be curtailed because of the difficult economic conditions?

If it were up to you to decide, would you be in favor of un-limited immigration or of curtailing it somewhat?

Do you think the public institutions (such as the Jewish Agency or the government) should decide whether immigration should be curtailed?

Seventy-eight per cent of the immigrants favored completely free immigration.

The items in "attitude toward ethnically mixed housing" were as follows:

In general, would you prefer to live in a house in which all the families came from your own country of origin?

If you could choose between an ethnically mixed house and a house in which all the families came from your own country of origin, which would you choose?

If you lived in a house in which all the families came from your own country, how would you feel about bringing one family from another country into a vacant apartment?

If you lived in a house in which all the families came from your own country, how would you feel about bringing a few families from other countries into some vacant apartments?

Sixty-nine per cent favored ethnically mixed housing.

LEVEL OF INFORMATION ABOUT ISRAEL

Three measures were used to estimate the immigrant's level of information about his new country. The first of these was a test of knowledge of Hebrew, in which the respondent was required to read at sight and translate into his native language eleven simple words. Nineteen per cent of the immigrants had a good knowledge of Hebrew (i.e., were able to translate seven of the eleven Hebrew words into their native language).

The second area was a simple test of social and political information. The items included were as follows:

Which is the principal spoken language in Israel?

Who makes the laws?

What happens to people who are openly anti-government?

Which political parties are now in the government? (The check list included a number of fictional parties for possible choice.)

What is the current policy toward the East and West blocs?

Fifty-four per cent were defined informed because they gave correct answers to three of the five questions.

The final test concerned knowledge of Israeli population problems and asked the following questions:

How many Jews are there in Israel now?

How many Arabs are there?

Is the city Ramle in Israel?

Is the city Tul Karem in Israel?

How many immigrants arrived in Israel in 1949?

Thirty-eight per cent answered three of the five items correctly.

None of the three scales used in testing for the level of information about Israel had intensity curves. The cutting points are, therefore, arbitrary, so that caution must be exercised in comparing the distributions on the information scales with other variables in the study in which the intensity function determines the cutting points.

Appendix B · Sampling Procedure

Sampling was carried out in two stages. First, a stratified sample of transit camps was drawn from the total list of camps; then, a systematic sample of adults from each camp was selected.

The first stage of the sampling was preceded by a geographical stratification of all transit camps. The camps were spread over a large part of the country; however, several camps generally clustered at one geographical point. The common practice was to group all camps at one location under one name, for instance, the Bet Lyd camp. At Bet Lyd, however, there were six separately administered camps, each housing some 2,000 immigrants. The six camps were called the Aleph, Bet, Gimel, Dalet, Heh, and Vav Bet Lyd camps. There were clusters of camps at Be'er Ya'acov, Pardess Hannah, Binyamina, Machaneh Yisrael, Rosh Ha'ayin, and Ein Shemer as well as at Bet Lyd. In addition, there were camps in and around Haifa and Jerusalem, although these were not so similar to one another as the other centers. Each geographical grouping had from two to six camps. By and large, the physical and social conditions of the camps in each of these locations were similar in housing, recreational facilities, crowding, isolation from the urban centers, and so on. The basic difference was an administrative one. It was, therefore, thought meaningful to consider them strata for the sampling process.

Single camps which did not fall into one of the strata were divided into three groups according to their populations. Camps with more than 2,000 residents were defined as "large"; with 1,000 to 2,000 residents, "medium"; and with fewer than 1,000, "small." Six isolated camps fell into these categories, two in each group. These three groups also served as strata for sampling transit camps.

It was decided that half of the camps in each stratum would be selected. In cases where the stratum included an odd number of camps, the larger number was selected. Camps were assigned numbers, and a random choice was made from each geographical or size stratum. In this manner, nineteen camps were chosen from the universe of thirty-five.

Because of the sudden budgetary cut toward the end of the field work, it was necessary to eliminate at the last minute the camps housing the Yemenite immigrants from the sample. At the time, there were 27,630 Yemenite immigrants in six camps. It is most unfortunate, therefore, that the population studied does not include any Yemenite immigrants.

Two other camps (Yavniel and Safed) which were very small and located in inconvenient, isolated districts were also eliminated for technical reasons during the field work. However, the size of the sample (thirty-six cases) to be interviewed in these camps made their elimination almost irrelevant insofar as the representativeness of the total sample population was concerned. The final result of eliminating the Yemenite camps and the two small camps was that fourteen transit camps remained. With these exceptions, the fourteen camps constituted a representative sample of all the transit camps in existence during this period.

The second stage of the sampling involved selecting the people to be interviewed in each of the camps. On the bases of the analysis planned and the type of statistical breakdowns that would be necessary to carry it out, it was decided to interview a sample of 3,000 immigrants. This constituted 3.7 per cent of the 81,207 immigrants then in the camps. The sample was divided proportionately among the strata of transit camps by determining how many cases constituted 3.7 per cent of the population of the total stratum and dividing that number proportionately among the camps that fell in the sample of that stratum. Thus, for example, in the Bet Lyd stratum, which had a total of 12,736 immigrants, it was necessary to interview 470 people. The three Bet Lyd camps in the sample had a total of 6,636 immigrants, so that it was necessary to interview every fourteenth immigrant. A systematic sample of every fourteenth case was thus drawn by name from the list of adult residents. This procedure was followed in each stratum of transit camps defined. The systematic sample was, of course, not always based on every fourteenth resident, but varied from every twelfth to every sixteenth, depending on the size of the population in the sample camps relative to the total population of the stratum from which it was drawn.

Eliminating the camps housing the 27,630 Yemenites reduced the total sample by over 1,000 cases (3.7 per cent of 27,630 is 1,022 cases). The thirty-six cases eliminated in the two small camps further reduced the sample, leaving a total of 1,942 cases to be interviewed. Finally, seventy-six cases could not be reached because of incorrect names or addresses or because of refusals. The last mentioned constitute less than 4 per cent of the final sample and resulted in a total population of 1,866 who were interviewed. Among these, the number of "no answers" varies, of course, from area to area in the questionnaire.

Index

Acculturation, 23, 28–29, 36–37, 117–138, 188–192
  definition of, 119–122
  scale items, 207–208
Activity, 165–170, 171–172, 193–194
Allport, Floyd, 59
Allport, Gordon W., 101
Anomie, 23–24, 181–182
Anti-Semitism, 158
"Approach" pattern of acculturation, 119, 125–126, 128–138, 188–192
Aspirations, occupational; *see* Occupational aspirations
Austerity, 18–20

Australia, 8, 46
  acculturation in, 126–128

Bartlett, F. C., 59
Bentwich, Norman, 16
Bettelheim, B., 80, 83
Boder, David P., 79
Bondy, Curt, 81, 83
British Mandate, 3–5, 15
Bruner, Jerome S., 58–60, 101
Buber, Martin, 4

Categorizing, 60–62
Class, 162, 164

Index

Cohen, Israel, 4
Cost-of-living index, 18–19
Crutchfield, Richard S., 58–59, 61

Decision-making, 48, 65, 183–184
Displaced-persons camps, 6, 18, 47, 80, 89
Dunner, Joseph, 3

ESCO Foundation for Palestine, 4, 15
Eisenstadt, S. N., 4, 71, 157
Emotional stability, 72–74, 77–78
Equalitarianism, 149, 157–159
Ethnic group, 177–181
  general grouping, 31–32
  number in sample, 31
  proportion in population, 41

"First Israel," 12, 118
Foldover technique, 195
Frame of reference, 59–62
Friedman, Paul, 86
Frustration, 64–68, 70–75, 186; see also Strain

"Getting ahead," 168
"Getting by," 168
Goodman, Cecile G., 58–60
Gruenbaum, Isaac, 4
Grygier, T., 26, 81, 101
Guttman, Louis, 39, 49, 86–87, 90, 95, 105, 195

Hachshara, 50
Halpern, Ben, 4, 46

"Hardening," 82, 84–85, 93–100, 187
Hebrew University, 38
Herzl, T.; see Post-Herzl period
Histadrut, 18, 87
Housing shortage, 7, 20–21

Ideology, 54–57
Immigrants
  countries of origin, 13–15
  demographic composition, 15–17, 40–42
  ethnic composition, 14–15
Immigration
  illegal, 5
  restrictive policy, 5
  size of, 6–7, 14
Information about Israel, 50–51, 53–55, 65, 68–71
  scale items, 208–209
Insulation by ideology, 74, 76–77
Intensity function, 195
Interviewing, 38–40
Isolation of immigrants, 11–13
Israel Institute of Applied Social Research, 34, 51

Janowsky, Oscar I., 4, 7, 11, 18
Jerusalem, 4
Jewish Agency, 11, 37, 87, 202, 208

Kahl, Joseph A., 168, 171
Kibbutz, 50, 144–146, 152, 161
Kibbutz Galuyot, 6
Kirman, Brian H., 101
Krech, David, 58–59, 61

Lehrman, Hal, 4, 18
Leighton, Alexander, 35
Lifton, Robert J., 83

Ma'abara, 7–10
Mandate, British; *see* British Mandate
Mead, M., 172
Merton, Robert K., 23
Morale, 36
  scale items, 203–205
  and unemployment, 104–113, 188–190
Murphy, H. B. M., 101

Nazi concentration camp, 9, 28, 79–103, 183, 187
Nazis, 158
  domination of Europe, 5
  persecution of Jews, 5
Niremberski, M., 80, 82

Occupational aspirations, 141–154, 158, 192
Occupational mobility, 147–148
  and employment, 164–165
Occupations
  attitude toward scale items, 196–198
  change of, 155–159, 171
  sons', 142–155

Passivity, 165–172, 193–194
Pioneering ethic, 157
Plans for settlement, 51–52
Post-Herzl period, 4
Problem-solving, 61–62, 184

Psychosomatic disturbances, 72–73, 77–78, 101, 132, 186

Quasi-scale, 90, 101
Questionnaire, 210–212
  languages translated, 38–39
  pretest, 39

Rationing, 18–20
Reference group
  comparative, 107–109, 187–188
  ecological, 109–112, 187–188
  ethnic, 29–32
Reinhold, Hanoch, 16
Relative deprivation, 129–131, 179, 189–191
Religious-secular balance, 76–77, 179–180, 185, 192
Reproducibility, 195
Richardson, Alan, 120, 127
Ripley, Herbert S., 81

Sacher, Harry, 4, 7, 11
Sampling, 37–38, 210–212
Scales, 39, 86–87, 105, 152, 195
  items, 196–212
"Second Israel," 12, 118
Secular-religious balance; *see* Religious-secular balance
Sherif, Muzafer, 59
Ship-to-settlement policy, 8
Shumsky, Abraham, 169
Shuval, J. T., 4, 157
Sibley, Elbridge, 162
Sicron, Moshe, 4–6, 13, 86
Social class, 162, 164
Social mobility, 155–173, 180–181, 191–193
"Softening," 82, 84–85, 93–100

Index

Soviet Union, 6, 8
Stouffer, Samuel A., 52, 72, 101, 105
Strain, 25–27, 181; *see also* Frustration
  response to, 27–28, 183
  types of
    frustration of expectations, 25, 88–89, 182
    unemployment, 25–26
    lack of assistance, 26–27, 87–88, 182
    prolonged stay in transit camp, 27, 89, 182
    family tension, 89–90
Strassman, Harvey D., 83

Taft, Ronald, 37, 117–118
Thompson, Lloyd J., 82
Tidy, Henry Letheby, 82
Transit camp, 7–8, 10–11, 22–27, 166, 182, 188
  ecological reference group, 109–112
  scale items, 198–203
  social relations, 35

UNESCO, 37
Unemployment, 9, 20, 142, 164–165, 182, 187–188
  and morale, 104–113
United Nations Special Committee on Palestine, 5

War of Independence, 17
White Paper of 1939, 5
"Withdrawal" pattern of acculturation, 119, 125–126, 128–138, 188–192
Wolf, S., 81

Yemenites, 15, 18
  number in sample, 31
Yishuv, 5
Youth Aliyah, 16

Zero point, 195
Zionism, 4–5, 9, 28, 45–48, 54–57, 64–65, 152–153, 183–186
  definition, 49–50, 67
  organizer, 183–184
  insulation, 184–186